Dr Fiona Vera-Gray is one of the UK's leading feminist academics working on sexual violence, and she has a decade's experience in the frontline anti-violence against women movement. Currently the Deputy Director of the Child and Woman Abuse Studies Unit at London Metropolitan University, Fiona was formerly at Durham University and has been a regular media commentator on pornography, sexual violence, sexual harassment and rape prevention. She is the author of two academic books on street harassment.

In March 2021, Fiona published the largest ever study on the content of mainstream online pornography, gaining significant media coverage, including the BBC, the *Guardian*, the *Sunday Times*, *New York Times*, and *Women's Hour*. She has been commissioned to write for the *Guardian*, the *Telegraph* and the *Independent*, and has appeared in both national and international documentaries about porn and its impact.

WOMEN ON PORN

One hundred stories.
One vital conversation.

DR FIONA VERA-GRAY

PENGUIN BOOKS

TRANSWORLD PUBLISHERS

Penguin Random House, One Embassy Gardens,
8 Viaduct Gardens, London SW11 7BW
www.penguin.co.uk

Transworld is part of the Penguin Random House group of companies
whose addresses can be found at global.penguinrandomhouse.com

Penguin
Random House
UK

First published in Great Britain in 2024 by Torva
an imprint of Transworld Publishers
Penguin paperback edition published 2025

Copyright © Fiona Vera-Gray 2024

Fiona Vera-Gray has asserted her right under the Copyright,
Designs and Patents Act 1988 to be identified as the author of this work.

A CIP catalogue record for this book
is available from the British Library.

ISBN
9781804995969

Typeset in 12.9/15.8pt Granjon LT Std by Jouve (UK), Milton Keynes.
Printed and bound in Great Britain by Clays Ltd, Elcograf S.p.A.

The authorized representative in the EEA is Penguin Random House Ireland,
Morrison Chambers, 32 Nassau Street, Dublin D02 YH68.

WOMEN

This book is for you.

*Abigail, Acacia, Alex, Alexandra, Alice, Ali,
Almina, Amelia, Angelica, Anita, Anna, Annabelle,
Annemarie, Arshi, Ashley, Aurelia, Beth, Billie,
Blair, Bonita, Carol, Catherine, Claire, Clare,
Daisy, Derrington, Diana, Dolores, Eleanor,
Elizabeth, Ella, Ellie, Em, Emma, Eva, Frances,
Grace, Hannah, Harper, Helena, Hester, Holly,
Imogen, Isabella, Isla, Isobel, Jade, Jane, Jay,
Jessica, Joy, Kate, Katherine, Kathy, Katie, Katy,
Kirsten, Kush, Laura, Leonora, Libby,
Lily, Louisa, Louise, Lubna, Luce, Maddie,
Maisy, Makeda, Marie, Martha, Molly, Myra,
Nell, Olivia, Polly, Prena, Rachael, Rebecca,
River, Rowan, Ruth, Sadie, Sam, Sara, Sarah,
Sherri, Simone, Siobhan, Sophia, Sorrel, Stacey,
Stine, Thora, Trish, Vanessa, Victoria, Violet,
Zara and Zoe.*

CONTENTS

PREFACE

IN 2005, THE AMERICAN AUTHOR David Foster Wallace gave a commencement speech to the graduating class at Kenyon College in Ohio. It started with a fairly innocuous story that went something like this: One fine summer's day, two young fish are swimming in the Atlantic when they happen to meet an older fish swimming the other way. They smile, nod their heads in acknowledgement, and the older fish nods back. 'Morning, kids,' she says. 'How's the water?' The two little fish swim on for a bit, reflecting on the interaction, until one turns to the other and asks, 'So, what the hell is water?'

Wallace's point was that the things that are the most obvious are often left unsaid; that the basic elements of our lives get lost in the background and can't be seen. Today, porn is a big part of that background. It's in our bedrooms, our boardrooms, our pockets, our Parliament. Though porn sites comprise just 4 per cent of the vast array of what's online, it's been said that they account for over 20 per cent of what we search for on our phones and close to 15 per cent of what we look for on our laptops. In fact, in 2021 the UK communications regulator, Ofcom, found that Pornhub alone had been accessed by 15 million people in the UK in just one month, mostly men but a significant number of women too.[1] It seems fairly obvious to say that porn is everywhere, but like the water, it goes mostly unmentioned. What is everyday is unremarkable, and porn has become our everyday. We don't talk about what we watch and what we don't, what we've seen, how we feel. And we talk even less about what it means for women. Or at least we have until now.

Seven years ago, I started talking to women about porn. Not porn as a political object, out there and for other people. But porn as a personal practice, what we do with it and what it's doing to us. From shaping our desire in ways that we can't quite put our finger on, to changing our relationships – including the one we have with ourselves – whether we found it or it found us, all women have a porn story. These stories might not sit well together, may rub against, contradict and dismiss each other, but together they make up the whole story. Or *a* whole story. This book captures one hundred of them, but there are millions more. We need to start listening.

INTRODUCTION

WHEN WAS THE FIRST TIME you saw porn? Late-night TV, a brother's hidden stash. Unasked-for messages in your DMs, unexpected pop-ups on your parent's computer. Even if you've never used it, chances are it has come to you. Though the routes to finding it change across decades, the fact that we find it does not.

I grew up in that generation who came of age on the cusp of the internet, all intermittent and unfamiliar. When I was thirteen, we got a second-hand computer with a dial-up modem that took five and a half minutes to connect to the internet just to cut you off when the phone rang. And the phone rang often because no one could text, or email, or voice note. There was no TikTok or Twitter or Instagram. No streaming either, no YouTube or Netflix. There were torrent sites for file sharing, but downloads were, at best, tem-peramental. In many ways porn was different back then; it felt smaller, more contained. But it still wasn't actually that hard to find, even if you weren't really looking.

Just before I finished school, I got a part-time job in a corner shop. We mostly sold cigarettes, milk and newspapers which were laid out with the magazines on a rack as soon as you came in the door. Every week along with lifestyle weeklies, we'd get a stack of issues destined for the top shelf. From lads' mags like *FHM* and *Maxim* – with covers that mostly blended into the rest – to titles like *Playboy* and *Penthouse* that stood out more, but not as much as you'd expect. I used to stock the shelves with porn back then in the same way I would restock the fridge. Unremarkable. That was probably the first time I encountered pornography but I can't say that I really saw it. It sat on my periphery, there but not there. It had to be pointed out before I actually took notice.

That happened when I was nineteen and living in a basement flat with a boyfriend. One day he was passed a battered VHS by a friend. I'm not sure of the process, if it was asked for or given, but I do remember what it was called. *Nothing Like Nurse Nookie*. A title to be proud of. It came home with him and sat for a week on the kitchen counter, before migrating quietly to a shelf in the corner. Looking back, I can't say I was particularly interested in watching it, but I wasn't that bothered by it either. Porn wasn't on the radar in the way it is now, or at least it wasn't on mine. So, the tape became part of the furniture, moonlighting as a bookend, a paperweight, a coaster, until one day, unprompted, we put it on. There was nothing ceremonious about watching it; it wasn't awkward but it also wasn't this shared special moment. It did pretty much what it was meant to do. I don't think we watched it again.

For years that was my relationship to porn, marked mostly by ambivalence. I've navigated sites by myself at different times for different reasons. Watched stolen content on the mainstream platforms, read some dodgy fiction. I've bought hotel porn with a partner back when that was what you did, and checked the search histories of men I've been sleeping with, not something I'm proud of but something I've done. I was never really that into porn, but I can't say that I never looked for it. The feeling would come, and I'd find something to watch but without really engaging in the process. I was half in it and half outside. It's hard to describe but it worked, for a while.

Then in my mid-twenties I started working in

a Rape Crisis Centre in London. It was the first time I really had conversations about porn, though they were never about what we might be watching. It was an unspoken assumption that women didn't watch porn, particularly women like us. If we did, it could only be feminist porn, the ethical kind, a world apart from the mainstream. But I knew for myself that wasn't the porn that I'd seen and I always wondered if it was the same for the others. We started running workshops in schools for young people, talking about consent, gender stereotypes, respectful relationships, and increasingly we found we had to address porn, mostly because the kids would bring it up. It meant we started creating a space to talk about porn's content and the industries behind it and this talking made my ambivalence harder to hold onto. The unease settled into something that demanded acknowledgement, something more solid: conflict. But when I looked around it seemed I was the only one who was walking this fine line with it all.

What pornography means for women is often split in two, with no room in between. On one side is the argument against porn. Here pornography is seen as exploitation, harming those involved in its production and society at large. Proponents point to an industry steeped in sexist, racist stereotypes that coerces performers and grooms users. Profiting from addiction, promoting violence. The evidence here seems to be growing. Former porn actors such as Jenna Jameson and Mia Khalifa have spoken publicly about an industry where women are sexually and financially abused, and an investigation by the *New York Times* in 2020 into trafficking on Pornhub led to the platform removing the majority of its content. But then there's another side which paints a more positive picture. Where performers are there because they want to be, because they love sex and are making good money. This is the argument that porn is more than one thing – pornographies not pornography. Queer porn, alternative porn, porn for every sexual appetite. Opening doors into sexual freedom, creating a space for us to challenge what we're told sex should look like or who gets to have it. Both sides of the story are compelling but they're also completely opposed, and so it's hard to talk about experiences that are somewhere in the middle; suspended in that conflicted space where we feel like, maybe, both sides are true. And that's where a lot of women sit.

What the polemic nature of the porn debates has meant is that there is hardly any room to talk about experiences of porn that might not be positive but aren't wholly negative either. We've been encouraged to bypass points of discomfort and contradiction, asked to choose narratives that are less complicated, where we are, perhaps, less implicated. It's hard to talk about watching mainstream porn and feeling worried about the wellbeing of performers, but not worried enough to stop watching. Or about supporting the idea of feminist porn in principle, but in practice getting more turned on by people who don't look like you, doing things that you're pretty sure would be painful. For women there's only two permitted narratives: either you're the cool girl who loves porn or the one who thinks it's violent. It's pleasurable or shameful, never a mixture of the two. And the consequence of all of this has been that most of us have stayed silent. At a time where women are more vocal than ever about what we want and what we do, there's an elephant in the room when it comes to women and porn. Most of us aren't talking to each other about what we do and don't do with it, and it means that no one is asking the questions that many of us are asking ourselves.

*

The legal academic Catharine MacKinnon, who famously drafted a civil rights ordinance whereby people in the USA could sue the state for being harmed by pornography – something that was passed in several cities before being blocked on the grounds of free speech – said in the early nineties that as pornography is about women, investigation into what it means should focus on what it means *for* women. Despite this, surprisingly little work has been done to start that discussion. When I say surprisingly little, I mean almost none.

When I started feeling this sense of conflict, I turned to research to make sense of it and found that women's relationships to pornography had been largely overlooked. In fact, at the time when I first started looking, the only study from the UK that focused solely on women was so dated that the definition for hardcore pornography was porn that showed an erection.[1] Sure, there were a couple of studies that asked women about using feminist porn, a few that focused on women's experiences of their male partners' use, and some that included girls in a study of young people. But the difficult questions, the in-depth questions, about what pornography means in the context of women's lives, the contradictions and inconsistencies, the complexities, were missing. Not just whether women are watching porn but why and what kinds, and if not, what's the reason? What are we searching for and what do we find? What do we think about it? How does it feel? What do women want to say on porn? I wanted to find some answers.

So, in the spring of 2017, I started talking to women about pornography. I began by thinking I would be lucky to interview maybe thirty women. I expected our conversations to be slightly stilted and hoped I'd have enough material to write an academic article or two. When the call went out over social media, over 200 women responded. It turned out women weren't silent because we had nothing to say. We were silent because no one had asked us.

Over the next two years, I spoke to one hundred women about porn. Across racial and class backgrounds, women from eighteen to seventy opened up in frank detail about what it has meant in their lives and how they feel about it today. Though the names of the women I spoke to may have been changed, what they told me has not. I've only fixed small details for clarity or removed parts that might identify them or someone else. Not everyone is quoted but my hope is everyone feels represented; though there was a range of different experiences, how these felt was often shared. We talked over the phone for sometimes close to two hours, our conversations starting with a simple question: when was the first time you saw porn? The candour with which women opened up about their lives was nothing like what I had anticipated. They told me about masturbating early and telling no one, about feeling unsure if what they did to themselves counted. Years spent thinking their role in sex was to perform, to convey their pleasure so a man could feel good. I heard about their relationships, break-ups and pregnancies. About having to contend with the role that violence has played in how their sense of sexuality developed. And many, probably most, spoke about a similar conflict to what I'd felt: a contradiction between what turned them on and what it said about women.

In writing a book called *Women on Porn*, the question of what we mean by 'women' is inevitable. Given my academic interests and the gap in the literature, participation was limited to women only. This explicitly included transgender and gender non-conforming women, though of the hundred women I interviewed, none identified as the former. I do wonder what would be thrown up in a study that focused more on these untold stories, a study that was more able to speak to what porn says about ourselves when we live at that intersection of being trans and being a woman. Researchers have argued, for example, that so-called 'trans porn' has moved from being a fringe genre to a mainstay of the big adult entertainment conglomerates. And Pornhub claims that in just one year the transgender category grew by 75 per cent, making it number two on the list of 'the searches that defined 2022' and the seventh-most popular category worldwide.[2] What might all this mean when it's your representation you're seeing? This book cannot speak to that, but my hope is that it will help those conversations to happen. For the women I did speak to, I was given an intimate window into their lives. And they gave me this, despite knowing that it would leave them open to judgement, because they felt like it was worth the risk. It was something that one of the women, Ruth, talked about explicitly in terms of connecting them all. She said she had a deep respect for everyone who responded, and those who – like her – shared their stories. 'It's taken something of ourselves to be able to be vulnerable and make contact,' she said. 'Knowing that there're others who might think differently to myself, but who are also open to look at it from another person's perspective.' She's right – I'm not sure I would have been able myself to share everything that these women have. I'm sure some felt defensive, unsure how they'd be represented, but they did it regardless. I hope I've done them justice.

Porn 2.0

When we think about porn today, we still mostly think about men. Men as the producers and the consumers. Women as the product. Now this may have been true a decade ago when the internet was still in its teenage years; a little temperamental and hard to rely on. But these days, with the internet in our pockets, technology has opened up access to pornography like never before. It means that while men are still pornography's main consumers, women are steadily catching up. Pornhub claims at least a third of its current user base are women, and a report from the Children's Commissioner in 2023 found a difference of just 16 per cent between how many girls said they had sought out porn – 42 per cent – compared to 58 per cent of boys.[3]

It also means that it's almost impossible to

comprehend just how much internet traffic is directed at accessing porn. A recent ranking of the world's most visited websites had three porn sites in the top twenty. And in 2020, Pornhub and X Videos were said to each receive close to 700 million visitors monthly – more than Netflix and even Zoom in the height of the pandemic. Along with social media and shopping, it seems that porn *is* what we do online. The global response to Covid-19 has only worked to increase this online domination, with a growing body of evidence finding a huge increase in porn consumption connected to the psychological and physical impact of lockdowns.[4] Even looking at just one site, the stats are overwhelming. Take Pornhub, the site that first comes to mind for many of us today when we think about porn. Founded in Montreal in 2007, Pornhub has carved out a particular space as the acceptable, almost default porn site. And it's one that, according to the company's own statistics, is visited by more than 120 million people each day.[5] In fact, in October 2021, when trouble at then Facebook HQ meant that Facebook, Instagram and WhatsApp were offline for several hours, Pornhub claims that traffic to its site increased by over 10 per cent – that's about half a million additional users for each hour that Facebook's services were down.[6]

Though seemingly just a passing anecdote, this increase shows how our use of porn has morphed into something almost unrecognizable. Where our porn use once was purposeful – we had to find space for ourselves, dig out the magazines, dust off the VCR – now it does the same thing as our social feeds; a source of mindless scrolling to help us pass the time. It's this change that meant, in 2022, a British parliamentarian was able to claim that he had just stumbled on the porn he was found watching in the House of Commons. Neil Parish was a Conservative MP who'd held the West Country seat of Tiverton and Honiton for over a decade but resigned after female MPs who'd been sitting beside him in Parliament raised a complaint about seeing him watching porn. Parish claimed it was an accident, that he'd been searching for tractors (he runs a farm) and had watched something on another website that had a similar name. He then admitted further to seeking out porn deliberately while waiting in the voting chamber. The idea of accidentally watching porn in Parliament or using it at work on purpose just to pass the time would have been unimaginable even ten years ago. But the changes in technology that have enabled it have accelerated a change in what porn is more broadly.

Back in the sixties, men like Hugh Hefner, the founder of *Playboy*, sought to create an idea of porn as an escape from the everyday. It granted exclusive access for men to a *bon vivant* lifestyle, where the whiskey was good, the cigars were better and the women were dressed like bunnies. This was an image of pornographers as wealthy gentlemen in silk pyjamas inviting other men into their world momentarily; a break from the bills, the kids and the nagging wife. Today, that's all changed. Enter Porn 2.0, which – like the general shift marked by Web 2.0 – emphasizes user-participation, ease of access and a seemingly endless stream of content. Gone are the bunnies and the sense of exclusivity, replaced by something more enticing: an infinite supermarket of unregulated content. When porn moved online and into our pockets, it not only increased our access, it removed much of the ability for individual countries to be able to legislate around it. This isn't about some tricky 'dark web' manoeuvring. The free mainstream sites that many of us access are able – legally – to show us material that would be unlawful for us to see offline. After all, the internet is global and most of the porn you access probably isn't hosted in the country where you live. This means that porn companies can use servers in countries with little regulation on pornography and you can stream it into your home even though what you're watching might be unlawful to buy in your country. And it's not just the content that is markedly different. Today's porn industry looks more like Silicon Valley than the Playboy Mansion, full of experts on algorithms, advertising and search engine optimization. Though the internet has provided some space for independent producers, the idea that it has somehow democratized pornography couldn't be further from the truth. These days porn is big business, led by a covert group of what can best be described as tech bros. It's also an industry that's been dominated for years by a company that until recently no one had really heard of. And that's the way they liked it.

In August 2023, MindGeek – the parent company that owns many of the world's most popular porn sites – changed its name to Aylo, citing the need for a 'fresh start' following some major controversies, and lawsuits, regarding the content on their platforms. The company had been bought earlier in the year by a private equity firm called – no kidding – Ethical Capital Partners, which has only existed itself since 2022 and looks to have no other acquisitions. Aylo might have a new owner, a new name and a slick new identity, but it still has a clear monopoly on the online pornography market. It operates an ever-growing portfolio of porn movie studios and platforms, including over one hundred pay-for-porn membership sites. It even runs Playboy's online and TV operations, though the Playboy.com site was bought back by Playboy 'at significant expense' in 2014.[7] But where Aylo really dominates is in the tube sites market. Here it owns dozens of popular free porn sites such as RedTube, YouPorn and, you guessed it, Pornhub.

If you haven't spent much time on these sites you might not be sure how they work. The sites function pretty much like an adult version of YouTube: all content is available for free, anyone can upload anything, and there is a system of ratings, number of views, comments and promoted content to encourage a sense of community. Users make money when other users watch their content so there is a financial incentive to keep on posting. The problem is that, unlike YouTube, most of these sites don't make any real attempt to prevent users from uploading pirated content. This means that a lot of porn on these sites is stolen, with the money being made going nowhere near the performers. The way that a few key players such as Aylo have cornered the market also means that performers are poorly placed to complain about their work being used without permission. Aylo not only hosts porn, it produces porn, sometimes a lot of it, under a range of different studio names which dominate most of the industry today. So if performers complain about their work being stolen and put on Pornhub for free, they risk being blacklisted by all of the studios that Aylo owns. Understandably that's not a risk many are willing to take. Aylo wants that free content on its free sites to encourage users over to its paid-for platforms. But even without this, the free sites themselves make the company more money than most of us are aware of. And in ways we've probably not really considered.

In 2020, a study of over 22,000 pornography websites found that 93 per cent of them were sending user data to at least one third party often without users knowing: Google alone was tracking users on nearly 75 per cent of the sites studied.[8] It means that though many of us think that porn tube sites like the portfolio owned by Aylo make most of their profits by selling space to advertisers, they actually make their money – like their social media corollaries – by selling something much more valuable: you.

These sites are collecting, cross-tabulating and analysing your data, then selling it on to companies to help them sell you stuff; the more they know about you, the easier it is to target their products right at your sweet spot. They're also mining the data themselves to understand and shape our behaviour, to keep us coming back. After all, the more users they have the more data they get, and the more return users they have the more detailed, and valuable, that data becomes. It's horrifying and fascinating in equal measure.

We're quite used to this model for other online companies; it's so common in fact that it has a name – surveillance capitalism – coined by Harvard professor Shoshana Zuboff.[9] This is the process of generating profits through the capture of personal information about consumers. It's crystallized in the often-quoted idea that, when it comes to the internet, if it's free, you're the product. Amazon, Twitter, TikTok and Facebook all function through highly sophisticated algorithms that target advertising, suggest relevant content based on our behaviour, and provide us with something that, once we've started using, becomes difficult to quit. What many of us are beginning to realize is the frankly alarming amount of information these sites can, and do, collect on us while we're aimlessly scrolling. Information which not only means that they can fairly accurately predict what we like, but they can also start to shape what we like, what we think and what we buy. If it didn't work, our data wouldn't be so valuable. And it's not just the detail of what we're looking at on that site that they're collecting, detail which for porn sites might be something we don't want to have shared. Often they can collect other information about what's on your device: your phone or computer's technical configurations; addresses of previous sites you've visited; things you've searched for; your location; even other pages you have open. This is pulled together with your activity on the site, not just what you click on but where your mouse goes, how long you stay there, how many times you return and when. All of this can be collected even if you are using private browsers, which help to hide your search history from others but do little to stop sites themselves tracking you.

If you're anything like me, you might figure that a piece of this information here or there isn't something to get too worried about. It can't really be that harmful, can it, to just accept all cookies? But porn sites can collect and pass on a whole lot of our data, and they're doing it with simply massive numbers of people. According to that same 2020 study, approximately half of the porn sites analysed had URLs that revealed a specific gender and/or sexual preference, identity or interest, and many of them were passing on that information without the user having any awareness of it at all. When this data is combined over time, and then brought together with all the other data collected over the sites that Aylo owns (remember the 120 million users daily for Pornhub alone), the resulting Big Data set can be usefully mined to influence attitudes, habits and ultimately behaviour. In effect it gives a map of how to sell anybody anything. And that's the real money shot. It turns out that far from the private access we think we've been given, online porn has actually meant that we're being watched a whole lot more. The same technology that's given us hashtags and trends, suggested people to follow, books to buy and opened us up to new sources of information, is being used to shape our sexual pleasures and practices with a clear profit motive for getting us hooked. So why is this important to know when we think about women and porn? It's pretty simple really: we've been a gap in their data.

The great divide

As the business model for online tube sites has become clearer, so too have attempts to fill this gap by bringing women in. While you might know the name Pornhub, you might not know that each year it publishes something called its Year in Review. These heavily infographic-based summaries provide a colourful round-up of user activity on the site over the past year, including the days and months the site was most accessed; the top searches, categories and videos; and the amount of time typically spent on the site (around nine minutes if you're wondering).[10] Though these annual reviews were first published in 2013, it wasn't until 2014 that they started providing specific information about women. This came out initially (and cleverly) through a collaboration with BuzzFeed, a popular website that focuses on producing viral content such as celebrity gossip and quizzes – the infamous 'blue and black' or 'white and gold' dress debate of 2015 helped catapult it into the spotlight. Collaborating with BuzzFeed like this meant that the findings could be circulated easily on social media without someone linking to the Pornhub site itself, creating a more palatable way of getting what is essentially marketing material out to a wider audience.

Titled '14 Things You Might Not Know About How Women Watch Porn', the clearly clickbait article was crafted to show women that porn wasn't something to be intimidated by. It included facts such as that Pornhub had a 'For Women' section, and that the nice and familiar Kim Kardashian was women's most searched-for 'porn star'. Back in 2014, Pornhub claimed women accounted for just under a quarter of its user base, at 23 per cent worldwide. Fast-forward to the Year in Review 2022 and now over a third of Pornhub users are women, making up 36 per cent of users worldwide.[11] Gone is the attempt to suggest that porn for women is different. In fact, the 'For Women' category itself has disappeared, replaced by 'Popular with Women', a smart rebrand that says a lot about the company's change in approach. The message now is that women watching mainstream porn is no longer niche; it's mainstream. And though we do need to take Pornhub's stats with a pinch of salt – the gender breakdown of users is based on Big Data, not users' own identifications and so there is room for error – we also can't ignore that this level of growth, on just one site, must be telling us something. But what?

Pornhub brings in New York City-based sex writer, educator and coach Niki Davis-Fainbloom to suggest the answer lies in gender equality. 'Women are feeling more deserving of pleasure,' she says. 'More women are feeling empowered, knowing that they deserve a WAP' – that's a 'wet ass pussy' – 'and exploring how the right video can help facilitate that for us.' This kind of explanation linking women's porn use to women's empowerment might be familiar – it often appears in arguments based on what's called 'sex positive feminism'. But that version of the story is usually not about mainstream porn sites; in fact, it often actively critiques them. A 2020 article from *Cosmopolitan*, for example, titled 'Women who watch porn have better sex', isn't talking about porn on Pornhub so much as encouraging women to seek out porn by one of the best-known feminist pornographers, Erika Lust – a woman who regularly and explicitly criticized Aylo back when it was called MindGeek, including by calling it 'an aggressive tech company' that only 'cares about traffic and advertising'.[12] But regardless of who is telling the story, the result is more or less the same. Women are divided into two opposing sides: women who watch porn, are empowered and having great sex; and those who don't watch porn and . . . well . . . aren't. The result isn't great for women, no matter what side you fall on. Not only is there still a stigma around women who watch porn, there's also an increasing pressure for women to watch it to prove that they're not frigid. It's something that the American singer-songwriter Billie Eilish spoke about candidly with shock-jock Howard Stern at the end of 2021.

Talking on Stern's radio show, Eilish detailed how she started watching porn when she was eleven, not because of her own desire so much as it being a way to demonstrate that she could keep up with the boys. Pretty soon, it became a personal habit. Her reflections on porn's impact are hard to dismiss – from the ways it distorted her view of her body to how it gave her nightmares and affected her sexual expectations and practices. She told Stern that it led to problems when she started having sex, saying that 'the first few times I had sex, I was not saying no to things that were not good. It's because I thought that's what I was supposed to be attracted to.' Essentially, she had learned a script from porn that sex was not for her to lead. So much for our WAPs. Relatively quickly Eilish was subjected to a backlash labelling her comments as being slut-shaming and whorephobic, with *Xbiz*, a well-known trade paper for the adult sex industry, claiming she had gone on a 'stigmatizing anti-porn tirade'.[13] She was also met with a response commonly pitted against anyone raising concerns about porn and its impact, namely that there are so many different kinds of porn that you can't really say anything about porn in general. Except Eilish wasn't talking about porn in general or going on a tirade about anything. She was talking about her own experience as a young woman with porn. And it's an experience that is legitimate, whether or not it matches our own.

Eilish created a rare space for young women to see another young woman sharing her porn story. But the response she got shows how hard it is to do that when whatever we say is taken as a judgement against those who feel differently. No one wants to open up when we know how women are pitted against each other. We're either too sexual or not sexual enough, sluts or frigid. We can never get it right. Shamed for what we do or don't do and scared our words will be hurtful to others, it means that no matter what we're saying when we talk about porn it's a tough conversation.

I've been acutely aware of this with the women I've spoken to and in the writing of this book. I don't want to add to the discrimination already faced by women in the sex industry, whether there by choice or coercion, or a combination of both. I don't want to contribute to how women are taught to judge ourselves and each other, to compare and compete, to always find ourselves wanting. But inevitably I will, because that's the only way we know how to have this discussion. Us and them. For or against. The great divide. We need to bridge it. Because without women talking about the realities of porn in our everyday lives, the good bits and the bad, we're passing the baton over to the big boys like Aylo to do it for us. What they'll say will serve their interests, not ours.

It's time we told our story.

DESIRE

Who women watch

IN 1973, JOURNALIST NANCY FRIDAY published the first, and still probably the most comprehensive, compilation of American women's sexual fantasies. *My Secret Garden* (not to be confused with *The Secret Garden*, incidentally a childhood favourite) was ground-breaking at the time for its shame-free discussion of women's erotic lives. Pitched by some as a clinical work, the book drew on hundreds of recorded interviews and letters from women Friday knew in her life as well as those who responded to adverts that she placed in various newspapers and magazines. But despite the inclination to think that her work was part of some bigger feminist project, Friday didn't locate herself as a feminist at all. She claimed in the book that the call of women's liberation in the seventies was too strident and had put women off, including herself. And I'm not too sure where she'd find her place post #MeToo given that in the nineties she appeared on a talk show arguing against the seriousness of sexual harassment because the workplace – in her words – was for both 'meeting and mating'.[1] In spite of this, her book stands out as a masterpiece in the literature on women's sexuality for its unshakeable honesty, its bravery and its simplicity. Though the understanding of pornography has dated and the text has been critiqued for universalizing from the fantasies of mostly white, heterosexual women, the overall argument is still compelling fifty years later. Basically, Friday claimed that a lot of our sexual fantasies are created to overcome the fear that wanting sex makes us 'bad girls'. Despite the social changes from when Friday was writing to now – the same year the book was published, for example, *Cosmopolitan* apparently ran an article that started with 'Women do not have sexual fantasies, period. Men do.'[2] – the prohibition on women's desire is still going strong. And it's something Makeda first encountered at the age of twelve.

As a child in the late eighties, Makeda had spent half her time in continental Europe and the other half at a boarding school in England, where she would stay with an aunty on weekends. She had two male cousins who lived there too, both older than her by a few years. Makeda said they all got along really well; in some way they felt like her brothers. They would listen to music, hang out and play games. They grew up together; it was like her second home.

She remembers a party at the house when she was twelve; an adult party where the kids got fed and were then sent upstairs to watch television. Makeda said that if you were a girl and you were quiet you could get away with hanging around a bit longer than the boys, who were just too boisterous and were sent up fairly quickly. So that night, by the time she got upstairs everyone was already watching telly. Except it wasn't telly. They were watching porn. 'It was the two boys at the house and then other boys who'd come with their family so there'd be six or seven of us in the room,' she said. 'And they were all fixated on it so they didn't even see me. I just snuck in and sat in a corner mesmerized by what was on the screen.' She sat there for a while – long enough to start to feel turned on – until one of the boys saw her and instantly everything changed. 'Suddenly someone said, "Oh, Makeda's here, you've got to turn this off." They all freaked and started asking me these questions like, "What are you doing here? How long have you been sitting there? Why are you watching it?" Then they switched it off, everybody disbanded and I went back downstairs.' The whole thing left her with the overwhelming feeling that what was on screen wasn't for her. 'It was clear,' she said, 'that the reason they were turning it off was because I was there, and I shouldn't be watching it because I am a girl.'

Makeda's experience crystallizes what a lot of women learn early on, not just about porn but about sexual desire. What she saw on the screen at that time amounted to her whole understanding of sex, and it was something being done to women to meet the desires of men. 'There was something else that struck me,' Makeda said. 'Because I was a girl I also felt embarrassed when the boys went out of the room. I felt embarrassed because that stuff was being done to women and I was a girl, a mini-woman. I was hoping that they don't think they can do that to me. The position of the women in the clips that I saw, they were there to service the men.' It's a powerful message to get at twelve and it's one that took decades for Makeda to overcome. It might be about us but it's clearly for them, not just porn but sex itself.

*

It was in recognition of the fact that most porn is made for men that the porn industry established the category of 'women friendly' porn. The idea is simple: if porn in general is made for men and by men, then women need to be invited in. Porn for women is exactly that. Though not necessarily made by women, it's supposed to be more representative of our desires. It's all about being softer, more romantic than the mainstream. Focused on sensation, silk sheets and flickering lights, dialogue and massages, and an awful lot of French kissing. It paints our sexuality as something wholly different to men's. Our pleasure, it says, comes from pleasing others; our desire is to be desired. And of course, that might be part of the story, but there's a whole lot it leaves out. The category itself has become increasingly controversial, with claims it simplifies our desires to one gendered lump and reinforces the idea that 'real' porn is for men. In many ways, though, the controversy doesn't matter, because when you speak to women about porn, it's not what we're watching anyway.

Annabelle was in her late twenties and had started watching porn in the last five years. She said that advances in technology had played a big part in that, plus the experience of her boyfriend moving away for university. But she'd struggled to find what she wanted to see, even though, on the face of it, what she wanted was fairly simple. 'For me as an audience or a user, I want to watch something where I genuinely believe that the woman is feeling pleasure,' she told me. 'Something where she isn't being put in a situation that she doesn't want to be in. But it's not just women; I want to see porn where the man isn't an object either. I can't stand those sorts of videos where the man is nothing more than a torso, a penis and the tops of his legs and that's it. Even if you see all of the woman she's still being objectified, plus he's nothing more than a mannequin at that point. I want to see that both of them genuinely enjoy it, because you can tell when they're faking it, or if it's just an act.'

It meant that, though she was straight herself, she told me she couldn't watch straight porn. It wasn't so much about a desire to see women as the desire to see anything that centred women's pleasure. She'd only found that in lesbian porn; she thought that to focus on the women, you had to remove the men. 'I can empathize with what happens in girl-on-girl action as something I'd like to have happen to me,' she said. 'It's the opposite of everything I used to worry porn would be. It's not aggressive, it's really sensual. Whereas in a heterosexual video he might do something for her but it's just for show. She then has to get on and do things for him. And if I'm trying to imagine it for myself, that's not what I would want to happen.'

In her mid-thirties, Acacia was a bit older than Annabelle, but said similar things about the kinds of porn she watched and why. Acacia started masturbating without porn – at her grandmother's house as a pre-teen – just watching shows on television with any kind of sexual content. It was when she first realized she could pleasure herself and explore what her body liked; what felt good to touch where. It wasn't until much later that she came across internet porn. For a while she was too scared to search for it, worried about what she might see, until a friend told her about RedTube (part of Aylo's portfolio) and she'd used that ever since – mostly for lesbian porn. 'I'm a straight woman,' she told me, 'but I enjoy watching women getting off so I watch mostly girl-on-girl where there is no man involved. For a woman to be with a woman, you know what you enjoy and what spots to hit. It doesn't mirror my own sexual life but I think I go to porn for the fantasy.' Like Annabelle, Acacia felt that when there were men in

porn, the women put on too much of a performance. She'd faked that kind of pleasure herself, so
when she saw it on-screen, it felt too familiar. She
said she had come to terms with the fact that sex is
not always going to be great for women; that sometimes you do it just because your partner wants it,
'so you make some more noise to end it, because
your partner's got off and you want to be done'. It
meant that, in straight porn, she felt able to see
through the show, and that took away the fantasy,
which was why she was there in the first place.

Ella also avoided heterosexual porn, but not
because of women's performance or pleasure. It
was more about what the men were shown doing
to them. Ella was twenty-four and had started
masturbating at seventeen. At the time she'd
experienced finding sex scenes in films exciting
and so thought she'd try to use some porn to help
her find out what she liked. But most of what she
found just turned her off. 'I think the first time I
looked at porn I was a bit embarrassed and over-
whelmed, if I'm honest,' she said. 'It was all
horrible and a bit sleazy or something. Just loads of
blowjobs and stuff that I didn't find arousing.' It
meant that she had ended up having an off-and-on
relationship with porn; she used it sometimes but

it felt like a struggle because of the sense – like Makeda – that it wasn't meant for her. 'I think because the industry is so driven by male views and male satisfaction it makes it difficult to find stuff where women's pleasure is a priority,' she said. 'You can go from thinking, "Oh, this is nice, seeing people having sex and enjoying it," to seeing something and thinking, "Oh, actually it's a bit grim. That woman seems like maybe she's being taken advantage of, doesn't look like she's where she wants to be, doesn't look like she's enjoying it." It's hard to find porn where women actually seem like they're having a good time." Enter lesbian porn. 'Quite early in my porn-watching days I found that looking for lesbian porn – even though I'm straight and I've never been with a woman and I don't intend to be – was a way of finding porn where there weren't men being violent towards women,' Ella told me. 'It would enable me to find things that I found arousing and enjoyable without that thing of watching a video and the woman starts getting grabbed by the throat.'

The kinds of porn that Annabelle, Acacia and Ella were watching often come up in statistics about how women use porn, but rarely is there any discussion of why. In 2014, Pornhub found that 'lesbian' was overwhelmingly the most viewed category by its female users – close to 150 per cent more likely to be searched for by women than men, and that 'girl-on-girl' porn was 445 per cent more likely to be looked for by women than men. In 2019, 'lesbian' was still women's favourite category, including in the UK, where we searched for it over 20 per cent more often than other women worldwide. By 2022 its popularity had only increased: 'lesbian' porn was now the most searched-for term by all users in the United States, and the most viewed category worldwide – perhaps reflecting a trend of more women accessing porn.[3] Though Pornhub doesn't provide much analysis about why women watch lesbian porn, it seems to have a lot to do with trying to see our pleasure being centred. Across the women I've spoken to, bisexual, asexual, pansexual and straight, watching 'girl-on-girl' on mainstream sites came up repeatedly in our conversations. In fact, the women who were actually the most critical of it were those who were – or thought they might be – lesbians themselves.

After identifying for years as a lesbian, Catherine came out as bisexual in her late twenties. Before that she said she never felt entirely sure of herself or her sexuality. It was a confusion that, in some ways, the mainstream picture of 'lesbian porn' had fed into. 'When I was in the process of coming out to myself, I was uncertain about what it was that I wanted. I wasn't really sure that I meant it, you know, or if I was just trying to be interesting by being gay,' she said. 'I have memories of searching out "lesbian girl-on-girl" pornography on the internet on our family computer at the age of thirteen and finding it vile because mainstream pseudo-lesbian scenes are just ridiculous. I was like, "OK, that's fine, I'm not gay. This is awful, I don't want to watch this," with no understanding of what went into the production of these things or who they were for.' Alexandra had a similar experience. She was eighteen when we spoke and fifteen when she started to question whether she might be a lesbian. She had seen a little bit of porn here and there, mostly from boys sending it as a joke, so when she started to wonder if she might be into women, it was one of the first places she looked. 'It was a hard time,' she told me. 'I was still going through school and exams and there were a couple of people who were out at my school but they'd get picked on. So, I was a bit scared because I was having these feelings.' She went onto Google, typing in things like 'how do you know if you're gay?' and pretty soon what came up were links to girl-on-girl porn on the mainstream sites. But when she looked, it wasn't what she expected and it made it harder, not easier, for her to realize who she was. 'All the girls, you could tell that they were staging it. They were all fully dressed up and had really long fake nails and I didn't identify with them at all,' she said. 'I am not a girly girl, or I wasn't at the time, and it made me feel like I didn't have a chance. You have an image in your head of what you think it is going to be like and then you watch something and it is not at all what you think. It scared the hell out of me because I thought, "My God, I am having these feelings but I don't think I could ever do what these women are doing."' Alexandra said she was really confused for a while as to whether or not she liked women in that way. Seeing lesbian porn had knocked her confidence, and that had quite an emotional toll. But then she left school and came out as bisexual, and felt in a much better place. She said she was finally starting to accept herself and not question what she wanted. For Catherine it had been a bit more complicated.

It wasn't just that Catherine was getting turned off by the lesbian porn she found, she was also turned on by some of the straight stuff, even when she found it problematic. 'At the same time as searching for lesbian porn, I remember putting serious effort into trying to find porn on very mainstream platforms and finding it unsatisfying and a bit gross but also a turn on and feeling quite guilty about it,' she said. 'I would go through these periods of quite intensively watching it for a couple of weeks and then feeling terrible and not doing it for six months. I cycled through that for a while.'

Then, when she was twenty, Catherine went to her first feminist meeting. 'I was at a lesbian-centric group and someone was arguing that the only pornography that was OK to watch was man-on-man, gay male pornography because no women were being subjugated,' she said. 'I remember feeling, "Yess! Here is permission I can go and watch sex and it's fine. I've been ethically sanctioned by the lesbian sisterhood." I remember that as a turning point.' So off she went to watch some gay male porn, found that she liked it and still uses it today. And much like the stats on women and lesbian porn, it seems as though Catherine is not the only one. In fact, Pornhub has suggested that, overall, women are 69 per cent more likely to watch gay male porn than the men it appears to be aimed at.[4] Leonora told me why she thought this was.

Leonora was a white lesbian woman who was in her mid-thirties when we spoke. She told me she'd been trying to rein in how much porn she watched online recently, and had gone back to reading – including Nancy Friday, which incidentally is where it had all begun. 'I'm thirty-five so I feel already weirdly like a dinosaur. I can remember pre-internet so my formative experiences with porn are with the written word,' she said. 'My parents had quite a lot of books and they gave me pretty unrestricted access. My mother had Nancy Friday and I remember reading that around twelve and just being like "Wow". That was a really positive thing, actually, because there was such a huge range. It didn't seem like there were many fantasies that were too weird or taboo, so I got pleasure from reading it but it was also really reassuring.' After starting out with books as a teenager, when porn moved online in her twenties Leonora's use moved with it. And what she found now was that she couldn't see her actual sexual desire represented without a whole lot of baggage that she didn't really want to deal with. 'The thing that's really frustrating to me as a gay woman is that there's no good representation of your sexuality in porn,' she said. 'If it's made in the straight world, it's gross and it's unbelievable. It just is not erotic, basically, to see women with super long fingernails scratching each other. And then when I watch porn, like the CrashPad Series, a type of feminist, queer porn that I watched a bit and I like the idea of, I just don't find it erotic. They've just got a bit of a worthy attitude and what I go to porn for, sometimes, is the darkness.' It meant that, like Catherine, Leonora discovered that gay male porn, though not ostensibly representative of her sexuality, was a way she could resolve some of the conflict she felt about how both women and her sexuality were represented in mainstream porn. 'I used to watch a lot of gay male porn, that was my go-to,' she told me. 'It feels dirty and it's hot but in a way that has a bit more parity. It basically removes the misogyny from porn.'

Maybe that's what sits at the heart of what – and who – we are watching. Not an attempt to see women in porn so much as a way to see porn without the way that porn sees women. It's this that is a big part of the driver behind the feminist porn that Leonora talked about watching. Though, much like her, for the women I spoke to, it still wasn't quite what they wanted.

What women want

Anna talked openly about her experience of porn, what she watched, what she didn't, and the problems she had with that category of 'women-friendly'. Anna was a White British woman who was now twenty-seven and had been using porn fairly regularly since coming across it as a teen. She first saw it on a site called Faceparty – a British social media site which enjoyed a brief heyday in the early 2000s. These days she sought out porn herself, though it wasn't the kind that's meant to be for women. 'In my experience,' she said, 'I've found "women-friendly" porn to be a bit limp-wristed. It's just so painfully dull. I feel like it's the result of a group of white male executives sat in a room asking the question "how do we make porn pretty?"' In contrast to the women-friendly stuff, Anna said she was a big fan of feminist and queer pornography. 'It's still raw fantasy, like dirty fucking, but there's a difference in the treatment of the actors and the shot,' she told me. 'It doesn't fall into the trap of: how do we make this tolerable for women? It's more an approach to constructing the image to have a balanced and authentic perspective.'

What Anna's talking about here is the idea of changing the way that porn sees women and it's an idea that's a mainstay of sex positive feminism. Though it took shape in the early nineties, the use of 'sex positivity' as a term can be traced back at least seventy years before that. It's a movement which takes as a starting point the idea that what we're told about sex is mostly all the bad stuff. We know about unwanted pregnancies and diseases, for example, but we rarely talk about the benefits. Like the fact that sex has been found by a number of studies to be an excellent form of pain relief, that it can lower your blood pressure and boost your immune system, help fight depression and anxiety, even extend your life.[5] In its basic form sex positivity is about trying to shift ourselves away from shame as our fundamental feeling about sex, and towards a much-needed focus on pleasure. We've got sex positive books, sex positive therapy, even a sex positive parenting style to help us talk about sex appropriately with our children. And at the heart of a sex positive position on porn is the recognition that – unlike the category of 'women-friendly' – we could make porn our own rather than just make it less someone else's. It's a call that's been put into action by producers of feminist porn. Feminist or independent porn directors, such as Erika Lust or Tristan Taormino, talk about producing pornography that challenges bad working practices in the porn industry and pushes back on the stigma surrounding women and sex. Performers are paid a fair wage, treated with respect, and their consent and safety are prioritized, even when what they are doing looks like a usual day on Pornhub. It's not about what's pretty but it does try to be more real. To articulate the range of what's sexy and sexual and counter the shaming of women. So far, so good. But though most women seem to support it in theory, in practice it's a different story. Even for women like Anna.

'It's fair to say that I'm not very good at being an ethical consumer when it comes to my porn habits. I'm lazy,' Anna told me. 'I generally want and try to be more ethical but it's hard when you're just looking for the quick fix of porn. Way too much content just seems to be based on showing as much skin as possible to turn a buck. One of my friends at school had a mantra for his porn usage: it's OK as long as I don't pay. It's like anything, price has an impact and if you can get content that does the job for free then why wouldn't you use that?' It turns out that, when you ask, most women who use porn are using the same old sites as men – the free, mainstream tube sites and the free, mainstream porn on them. We might be navigating around them to find something that centres women's pleasure, or – like Leonora and Catherine – something that avoids women completely. But we're using them nonetheless. It might be the truth, but it's not the message that most of us get.

In 2022, *Marie Claire* published an article promoting porn for women. It listed thirty of the best female-friendly porn sites. Most of them would be classed as feminist porn and for pretty much all of them you needed to buy a subscription. While it's good to get the message out that other kinds of porn exist, the problem is the way that this is used to cover over the fact that it's not 'other kinds' that most women are watching – even by data that *Marie Claire* itself has collected. In 2015, the same magazine had run a survey with its readers about their porn use with over 3,000 people responding, 91 per cent of whom were women.[6] Readers were asked to select from pre-defined answers on things like whether they use porn alone or with a partner, what devices they use, and how they feel about it. And though they weren't asked specifically about independent, queer or feminist porn, a clear three quarters said what they accessed was free, which most of this kind of porn isn't. What's happening here is a contradiction between the public story of what women use and the mainstream free pornography that the majority of us are actually watching. It can leave us feeling like we're out on a limb when actually what we want might be more common than we think. It's implicated in some of the silence around women and porn. It makes it harder to say what we're actually seeing because nobody wants to be the odd one out.

Prena was a lesbian woman in her mid-twenties and had been using porn since her early teens after stumbling across sex toy sites and using them to masturbate until she found the real thing. A few years after that, she moved on to using the free mainstream porn sites. But then Prena decided she wanted to try something more upmarket and told a friend she wanted porn for her eighteenth birthday. To her surprise he got her a DVD. 'I joked about him buying me some lesbian porn,' she said. 'I think by that point I knew that I was more into girls and I'd searched around online for lesbian porn and realized that it really wasn't turning me on. It was just straight girls slapping each other's boobs and I wasn't into that. I didn't think he was going to take it seriously and then he did, so I got some actual good-quality porn, which was a nice treat and I still have it now.' She told me it was officially 'feminist porn' and it seemed more realistic, as if the women were genuinely into it. But she also said that while she liked it enough, it was missing something that those other sites had, something a little more basic. 'I do feel like there's a side of me that's a bit tackier and disgusting, that just needs more vulgarity and I don't know what that's about,' she said. 'I don't know how much of it is socialized and how much of it is a visceral need for something to be almost smashed together, like an aggressive action accompanied by aggressive noises and this sense that the more aggressive it is the more they must want each other. I never really imagine myself as any of the people in the scenarios, so it's not that I want myself to be taken, like, ravaged by this man who needs me so badly, and I also don't want to do that to someone else. But I do definitely want to see that and I'm not sure what that is. I don't know how to put it any other way but I need almost a hint of non-consensualness to make it sexy.'

What Prena's talking about here connects to what Leonora called the 'darkness', and what it means for women's desire became almost impossible to ignore following the phenomenal success of *Fifty Shades of Grey*.[7] Though it came out over a decade ago, the series was still a reference point for many of the women I spoke to, and for good reason. Dubbed 'mummy porn' by the mainstream media, the popularity of *Fifty Shades* is almost unimaginable. In just one year, E. L. James went from being an unknown self-published author to a multimillionaire with the fastest-selling paperback in UK history. At the height of its success, two copies were sold every second, and at one point the UK ran out of silver ink, thanks to its use on the cover. All of this was despite the fact that even man of letters Salman Rushdie said he'd never read anything published that was so badly written. From descriptions of desire as pooling 'dark and deadly in my groin' to the statement that cold orange juice 'makes my mouth a much better place', the quality of E. L. James's writing has come in for some pretty heavy criticism.[8] But like it or not, the series started a conversation on the nature of women's desire that hadn't really been had before or since, or at least not so publicly.

Though she was in primary school when the books were first released, Lily talked about their impact on women's sexuality. She was in her late twenties now, and stayed mostly away from porn after boys in her early twenties had used it to try to intimidate girls; it was how they staked their territory. 'At university we were in a mixed shared house and porn was used in a teasing way to embarrass us,' she told me. 'The guys would find very gruesome or violent examples to share in order to make us feel uncomfortable. It was assumed that porn wasn't something we talked about as girls; it was something we were supposed to be horrified by.' Lily thought that the basic storyline of *Fifty Shades*, persuading a reluctant but secretly ravenous woman to participate in the kinds of sex that aren't for good girls, flooded a lot of our media; that the story itself wasn't unique, though not usually framed within a plot that includes red rooms, whips and blindfolds. 'There's only a certain kind of sexualized content that's acceptable for women to appreciate, like the *Fifty Shades of Grey* film where there's that power angle to it. It reinforces the idea that sex is a service you offer men,' she said, 'rather than something you participate in and even enjoy or would choose. Eventually, in mainstream film, that does turn into consent, but it's a reluctant or delayed consent which is seen as more desirable than a woman who actually wants it.'

Back in the seventies, Nancy Friday argued something similar. She thought that the idea of rape does for a woman's sexual fantasy what the first Martini does for her in reality: relieve her of responsibility and guilt. This might be behind the fact that women's reluctant consent is sometimes seen as more desirable, not just by men but – like Prena – for us too. It's a way that we can want without wanting, a means to escape the blame put on women for being sexual. Though on one level it seems to make sense, when we dig a bit deeper it gets messy. There are studies finding that men fantasize about 'forced sex' more than women, for example, and others suggesting that many of the people who fantasize about being dominated also fantasize about dominating others.[9] These days it also isn't without its complications because not everyone's guilt is relieved. Particularly when we're watching our fantasies of submission and non-consent play out on the bodies of other women online.

Violet was in her late thirties with a successful career in the theatre. Like Leonora, she started off using written not visual materials as porn. The first thing she can remember properly fantasizing with was the follow-up to *My Secret Garden*, Nancy Friday's *Women on Top*. 'I came across a copy and bought it and then would use it as material to masturbate to,' she said. 'I'm sure Nancy would be horrified to be thought of as porn but I wouldn't read any of the analysis between fantasies, I'd just read it because it was arousing.' For a long time, Violet stuck mostly to that; reading things felt more private and it allowed her more room to put herself in the picture. But one day she was horny and thought she'd see what was online, going first to XVideos, the world's most visited free porn site, and then a BDSM, fetish and dating site. She never really looked back.

Violet was very open about what she looked for in porn, searching mostly for anal sex with lesbians or with men and women. But she was also open about sometimes feeling a sense of internal conflict. She told me she found it interesting being a feminist who enjoys submissive sex, intrigued by the politics behind that. It was something she'd thought a lot about and still felt quite unresolved, particularly when she was watching it in porn. Because though she might want to see what's happening for the women in it, she could never be sure that they wanted it too. 'I'll be turned on by seeing something where a woman is in a submissive scenario and there might be a level of aggression,' she said. 'But then also thinking, "Fuck, this isn't good." It's both troubling and arousing for me. I feel like it's important to say though, if I'm watching something which is just too much, like too hardcore in terms of human rights, I stop watching it because I feel too uncomfortable about it. I've stepped into a territory I don't want to be in.'

Violet acknowledged that there was more than one route into porn for women, and these days with the access provided by the internet arguably there are ways to have more control. But her desire to see women's submission gave her a sense of conflict not relief, because unlike reading Nancy Friday, now the things that she was fantasizing about were being done to real people. It's a conflict that I heard in what a lot of women told me. It wasn't driven by a morality or breaking social taboos. It was based on what arouses us and what it means for women.

Playing with the borderline

Sherri was a Black British woman in her late forties and mother to three almost grown-up children. But back when she was twenty-four and a single mum with two toddlers, she was approached one day by a man in IKEA and asked if she wanted to pose for some photos. 'He followed me down the aisle and told me how great I looked. And then he asked if I wanted to come work for him. I said, "Doing what?" and he said, "Having photographs taken to go into pornographic magazines."' Sherri told him sorry, but no. So he decided to up the ante. 'He said, "Would you be interested in making films, then?" and I asked what kind and he said, "Porn." I said no again but he kept going on about how gorgeous I was and how much money I'd make.' On the one hand Sherri was shocked by the conversation they were having – it's not something you expect when you're out shopping for flat-pack furniture. But on the other, she said she was intrigued, which is why she stopped to listen. Working in the sex industry had never crossed her mind. It wasn't something she would have ever sought out for herself, but she had hardly any cash and felt a bit desperate. It could have solved a lot of her problems; it wasn't a choice she had wanted but now it was in front of her, it was hard to turn down. 'I'm a single parent with two young children, struggling with my bills, and someone approaches with this proposition, it's just so close to home,' she said. 'If I'm honest with you I almost went there; the money was too enticing. At the time it was something like £150 for the pictures, £300 for the movie. I thought, gosh, I could pay my bills and have money left to buy my kids the stuff they need.'

She ended up taking his number and met him in a café a couple of days later. After talking it through she thought the money wasn't worth it and never called him back. Reflecting on it now, she thought it had shown her the inequality in porn; that the starting points were different even if it ended up the same. She said she could have been exploited and violated; it could have turned really nasty, and she would have been stuck in something quite simply because she was a woman with no other options. It changed how she felt about the porn that she'd watched. 'I have an insight into the other side and how people could potentially get started in it, that's what really made me think that porn's just not for me,' she said. 'I understand that there are women that do it because they find it enjoyable, but how many are in a situation like I was, and are doing it because they feel like they have to? They feel they have no choice but to do it to survive.'

The experiences of women in pornography are the source of much heated discussion. On one side are the stories of empowerment, both sexual and economic, on the other stories of exploitation, of trafficking, grooming and violence. There are women who have had private sexual images stolen, 'leaked' videos compromising consent in amateur porn, and women who have set up successful careers from professional shoots or webcams. There is no single story. The knowledge of this sits behind the conflict that women can feel about the porn that they watch because we know that both versions of the story could be true, but we can't know which one we are watching.

Rowan was almost forty when we spoke, a white woman who'd gone through the gamut of porn, from casual use to something that felt like addiction, culminating in a complete rejection. She told me about masturbating in the exam room during her GCSEs because she was frustrated – 'just crossing my legs with my thighs together to get off'. It was something that's never part of the story about why women masturbate; that it can be quite functional and we can do it in multiple ways.

A few years after she'd finished school, Rowan got hooked on porn. It started when she found what her father had been using and escalated into something she found hard to stop. 'I was looking at my dad's history on his laptop one day and I saw something, a search engine thing that played various bits of porn every day,' she said. 'It's all presented to you and it's all free and, although I wish it hadn't, it gave me the idea. So, then I just used that link and every day it gave me a selection of porn that I could choose from. I was looking up things like anal, threesomes, whole groups. I never really looked for things that were nicely made by women. It was always pictures of women really being abused in some ways, being penetrated and controlled by men. All of it was humiliating, I have to say. I was trained to find those things arousing, so sex to me was about women's humiliation.'

Rowan said it affected her self-esteem. That all through her twenties she thought her value came from what her body looked like and how good she was at sex. And even though at the time, watching it was what she wanted, she started to notice a feeling that wasn't about pleasure creeping in. 'After I'd orgasmed watching porn, I would think, "Never again, that's horrible, why did I do that?"' she said. 'I felt bad about what I was watching, not dirty myself, but bad. I'd wish I hadn't watched that because I didn't want to be turned on by what was being done to those women.' It was something Prena had also told me; that there was a difference in feeling between how she felt when she was getting off compared to seeing what she was watching after she'd come. She said there was a threshold where she'd stop what she was doing, but that threshold changed depending on whether she was still turned on. 'Often what I would consider fine, while I'm watching it, as soon as I've orgasmed, if it's still on, I'm disgusted,' she said. 'I think things like, "God that woman just really doesn't look like she's enjoying it," and I need to get rid of it straight away. I definitely have a line where it's gone past my threshold and I'll turn it off. But the line is different depending on whether I'm masturbating or not.'

Rowan said that she tried hard to put that horrible feeling out of her mind, to rationalize it. She said that if she thought too much about it the guilt would stop her from watching and she wanted to keep doing it because masturbating like that felt good. For almost ten years she was in this loop, not telling anyone what she was doing. The conflict was working to keep her quiet, and keep her watching, just like the sites wanted. Until one day her sister saw what was in her browser. 'The only person that ever said to me, "Are you sure you really want to be watching that?" was my sister,' Rowan told me. 'She's allowed to say that because we're close and that really did help. Having someone say that to you is so powerful. It felt like I'd been witnessed.' The question came from care, not judgement, and it gave Rowan the space to ask it herself. She decided she was going to try going back to her imagination, which was hard at first but, like a muscle, it started working again. After that her porn use started dropping until she realized that she hadn't looked at it for weeks. And then for months, and then for years, until she didn't look at it again. She told me it wasn't difficult, but if her sister hadn't brought it up, she's not sure where she'd be. 'The shame and taboo keep it secret so nobody can ever challenge it or discuss it,' she said. 'The guilt and the shame stay tucked away. It's such a nasty trick.'

You've probably heard the argument that humans have always used porn, usually brought in to defend against any critique of what we use today. Human beings may have always sought out sexual stimulus but that's pretty far from what's on our screens. Researchers have coined the term 'panicked arousal' to talk about what it feels like on a lot of these mainstream sites.[10] It's not about stimulation so much as overstimulation; a constant carousel of images meant not just to arouse but to overwhelm, no matter what you were looking for in the first place. Annabelle, who'd said she only watched 'girl-on-girl' porn, talked about being interrupted as she searched for it by all the other content on the mainstream sites. 'It's the ads,' she said, 'the ones that say so-and-so from three doors down from you wants to fuck and there's a picture of a woman with enormous boobs, and you think, that is so contradictory to what I've gone looking for.' Lily mentioned the impact of the same kinds of pop-ups when she first looked at porn, long before the boys at university used it to try to embarrass her. She saw the ads as a form of intrusion, and said that regardless of what she was looking for it was this that contributed to that troubling feeling. 'I see it as the digital version of a flasher in the park, almost this violation. Even though obviously it's advertising and it's all about the revenue, it does feel like it's taking advantage of your vulnerability,' she said. 'I don't know whether I would have felt that at the time or even if I would have understood the angle of power aspect but I certainly felt ashamed that I had witnessed or seen it. Even though there was no autonomy whatsoever, there's still a sense of shame.' It was because of all this that Ashley said it would sometimes take her hours to find porn she could use. And even then, she was still left conflicted – her desire confused by what she'd seen trying to meet it.

Ashley described herself as 'a fairly old twenty-six'. She was a mixed-race woman who told me that she first saw porn at ten years old when she stumbled across a pornographic cartoon online. At the time it felt naughty but also a bit arousing; it was actually really confusing as, being animated, it seemed like it was meant for someone her age. She knew it was porn, though, and that she shouldn't see it. It felt too mature, like it was over her head. From that point to when she was eighteen, she'd see porn intermittently. It was only when she got a laptop for college that she started to access it herself. These days she used the mainstream porn sites and tried to navigate them as best she could. But that was hard because of how the sites are set up and what it meant for what she saw. 'Being a millennial, you grow up in a mad hypersexualized culture, so you're always a little conflicted,' she said. 'It's like I'm kind of turned on by this but I also know it's smutty and wrong and that's what I get from porn. When I have gone to look for porn online, I have to scroll through these horrible videos and get bombarded with these adverts, and they go against my core beliefs of not exploiting women in any way. But it's like two overwhelming sensations of feeling quite disgusted but then feeling really horny as well. It's a very conflicting path you go down; it feels like a delicate dance.' Ashley told me it meant that there'd been times where she'd spent ages looking for something she could masturbate to, by which point she wasn't even really horny any more but she'd invested so much time she wanted to follow through. She'd heard this described as a 'bully wank' – when it doesn't matter what's going on, you grit your teeth and finish yourself off. But it also meant that some-times she'd just come to whatever was in front of her, and that meant that she'd orgasmed to some pretty unsettling images. 'Sometimes I'm just about to have an orgasm and I've worked my body up but my mind has started seeing some-thing that's not cool. I'm stubborn enough to finish the task at hand and that is what I've done,' she said. 'I'll think, "Oh that's really bad, but look, I'm in this now. I might as well just finish it to make it worth my time." I can't believe I'm talking about everything so openly, but I guess this is important, this is what we need to do.' The conflict for Ashley wasn't just in her mind, it was held in her body; in pleasure itself.

In her mid-thirties when we spoke, Kush was a bit older than Ashley and she talked through what she'd learned about this delicate dance and the dangers of it. She told me she'd started watching porn over the past decade or so, when she'd got her own laptop and was able to do things a little more privately. There were things she would watch and some things she wouldn't and a couple of mainstream sites she would visit. Overall, she felt quite resolved in the porn that she used except every now and then she'd click on a new category to find out what's in there. This is where that conflict came in for her, together with a sense the site was trying to test her boundaries. 'A couple of times I've been disgusted by myself, by some of the things that I've found turn me on,' she said. 'Say, I'm watching a woman gagging on a man and being slapped in the face, I'm disgusted but I'm turned on at the same time. I don't like the fact that it's brought me to those two places in equal force.' She thought it was about toying with the boundaries of your morality – what Violet said about finding yourself in territory you don't want to be in. Kush told me that she thought it was a dangerous game, playing with that borderline of your principles versus your desire. 'I think if you push it too far, or if you get used to crossing that border, you can lose yourself,' she said. 'We've all got our own boundaries, we've all got the place where we're willing to push. And for me, I'm not willing to stretch it that far. I have to keep something about me.' As a Black woman Kush said she had a responsibility not to ignore certain things, that anything happening to a woman who looks like her is her problem. It's a powerful principle to ground us, but one the porn sites themselves make it hard to hold. It was also something Zoe mentioned in an almost throwaway comment that posed a way of looking at mainstream porn that I'd never heard before.

Zoe was a Jewish artist in her twenties and one of the few women I spoke to who paid for the porn she watched. She'd got a subscription to Erika Lust a few years ago, mostly because she was concerned about what was going on for the women in the porn on mainstream sites. 'There was a time when I was getting into porn where I'd browse free streaming websites like RedTube or YouPorn, but I just didn't enjoy what I found on there because it's objectifying and it feels quite fake. There's just something seedy about it,' she said. 'I guess it's this feeling of like, "Who are these women? Why are they doing this? Do they want to? Do they have options? Are they being treated well on set or is it just this guy fucking her and all these guys telling her what to do?" Whereas I watch Erika Lust films and I'm like, "These women have the best lives ever," like they're doing something because they love it and it makes them feel great and powerful and pleasured.'

Zoe said she was a sex positive feminist and didn't judge what women wanted to see. But she was critical of the content on mainstream sites, including what it literally said about women. 'It's the wording around porn that's important too. It's one thing if you search "I want blowjobs" or "I want threesomes" but when it's like "Fat sluts riding dicks" it's just all quite aggressive,' she said. 'You go on these pages and there'll be a pop-up of a thrusting dick in your face, gifs of "Watch this slut mum get fucked" and it's like, this doesn't make me feel good, this doesn't make me feel sexy, this doesn't make me feel like these websites are for women. It's not the kind of porn where you feel pride about what you are doing. I think that actual porn on those sites is directed towards shame.'

Zoe's point is subtle but it changes who we look to as the cause of the conflict. The idea that the porn itself leads towards shame and the sites are leading us to it. Think back to Aylo and the data that it collects and combines to shape our online activity; what if it is using some of that to push us further than we want to go? Not to help expand our sexual repertoire so much as to actually bring about some of this internal conflict. A recent study conducted on tracking on Pornhub found the site significantly segments, distributes and manages content and the layout of that content based on the profiling of its users: adjusting what we see to what it's learned – from the huge data set it has – will keep someone like you on the site for longer.[11] In reality, no matter what you're doing on these sites, you are being spoon-fed a limited range of content based on the keywords you use, your geographic location, the site's algorithms and the information that they're processing from the cookies on your browser. It means that a lot of the conflict we might feel is coming from what's being brought to us; content that is designed not just to be arousing but also to pull us towards something more extreme.

In his Reith lectures series for the BBC at the end of 2021, Professor Stuart Russell – a leading researcher in artificial intelligence – described in fascinating detail how content-selecting algorithms like those on social media, and on porn sites, work.[12] What he says gives fairly firm evidence that porn platforms have a profit motive for moving us towards content that we probably wouldn't choose ourselves. The algorithm's objective, he says, is simple – it wants to maximize click-through; it is programmed to get the user to click on what is presented, by whatever means possible. And though we might think people are more likely to click on what they already like, what content-selection algorithms have learned is that it is more useful to push users towards increasingly extreme content. This is because it has learned that users with more extreme preferences are more predictable. More predictable users are better for click-through, so to make us more predictable it tries to make us more extreme. It's part of the reason why it can seem like everything – from political views to personal preferences – is being increasingly pulled apart into binary camps at opposite ends.

It's not an accident or coincidence, it's part of the online business model, and many of the big porn sites are in on it. It means that the porn we watch might not be reflecting our desire so much as directing it towards what makes the most profit. It's guilt-by-design and it keeps us quiet, all the while coaxing us further in than we might really want to go.

When we spoke, Makeda had come far from being that twelve-year-old girl in the corner. She was a successful Black British academic, a mother to a much-loved son, and a woman who talked slowly and thoughtfully about sexual desire as well as the conflict that sometimes came with it. 'I have no shame around my use of porn in a general sense,' she told me. 'But I also don't really like it. I think that the way that women are portrayed is, for the most part, disgusting, offensive and ought to be wiped off the face of the planet. I guess I have a love/hate relationship with most of the porn I watch, but that doesn't stop me using it.' For Makeda, sitting with this conflict was part of her journey around desire; a journey she described as relaxing into herself and accepting all that comes with it. 'I'm seeing that some of the things that turn me on are against my principles or my political position,' she told me. 'But that's the thing about desire, it's messy and complicated. It's human.'

Sigmund Freud apparently once said that in his thirty years of research he'd never been able to answer the question 'What does a woman want?' It's an image of our desire as mysterious, an enigma, unknowable even to ourselves, and it's been hard to shake. But the problem might have more to do with the question itself rather than saying anything about us. After all, as women, we're more than one thing and so is our desire. Some porn is for us but not the kind that we're using, and we might want equality but fantasize about submission. The messages we get are a mess of contradictions. No wonder there's no one way through it.

BODIES

Judging ourselves

SORREL GREW UP DURING THE seventies in a big Caribbean household in the north of England. One of two girls in a family with four boys, she learned early on that not only was her vulva not to be looked at, it wasn't even something she could name. 'My mother never called it a "vagina",' she told me, instead 'it was called a "munchie". We weren't allowed to touch the munchie, we weren't allowed to see the munchie, and we definitely weren't allowed to speak about the munchie.' In this, Sorrel and her munchie aren't alone. No matter what we call it, many women grow up with the sense that there's something unspeakable 'down there', and it shows. A poll of the British public in 2019 found that 46 per cent of women mistook the vagina for the vulva, something I've definitely done myself, as did some of the women I spoke to. The vulva encompasses our labia, clitoris, and vaginal and urethral openings – basically everything we see if we go looking – whereas the vagina is just the name for the birth canal. And we're not only confused about what things are called. In 2021, a group of health researchers in the UK found that half of those surveyed didn't know where the urethra was and, regardless of gender, over a third couldn't locate the clitoris. In case you think there's something particularly British about all of this, in 2010 an advert by the tampon company Kotex was banned by three of the major US networks just for saying the word 'vagina', and a recent poll found that roughly half of US women couldn't identify the cervix or the uterus.[1] Part of the reason why there's so much confusion might simply be biology; the very nature of the female body means it takes effort to have a look. We need mirrors, torches, particular positions. It's purposeful, you need intention. But the ready availability of all kinds of pornography has given a level of access to women's naked bodies that we've never had before. What is that doing and what does it mean for how we feel about our own?

*

Luce first saw porn at eleven after a friend sent her an email of a cartoon comic book series that essentially ended up in a massive orgy. 'It was silly, funnily drawn like cartoons are, but I remember being quite shocked by it. I think that was the point,' she said. 'You thought you were just looking at a cartoon and then it turns into this completely graphic, sexual thing. I remember being taken aback by it but then also noticing the reaction in my body; I was turned on at the same time.' She said she felt a bit embarrassed, like she was supposed to find it funny and not arousing. So, she shut the feeling off and didn't think about it again, until she saw porn through her male friends at fifteen. 'At that age we started going on chaperoned trips away with our friends, camping and things like that,' she told me. 'I remember a couple of times guys having a porno magazine, that might have been the first time that I'd seen really graphic pictures of women sitting with their legs apart. Cameras right at the vulva kind of thing. I think that was the first time I'd seen that kind of stuff because at that point the internet was just in my parents' house on our slow computer and there was no way I was going to go there.' This time, however, Luce didn't feel aroused. Instead, she felt anxious about her body, specifically her vulva. 'I remember being really nervous about what my vulva was like compared to other people's,' she said. 'Because I'd never really seen somebody else's before and I had no idea what they were like. I'd never done the whole using a mirror to see what you look like. I didn't even really know what I looked like from that angle. So, suddenly seeing photos of vulvas was terrifying because I couldn't quite tell what was normal.'

It was years later when we spoke; Luce was approaching thirty and had been using porn herself for years. She thought it had helped her explore her sexual desire, given her permission to experiment and figure out more about her sexuality. But some of its impact on her body had never quite gone away. 'The women that I see in porn have a very specific look; they have these very fit bodies and these perfectly waxed vulvas and everything is hairless,' she said. 'The worst thing for me is the inevitable comparison that I sometimes give myself physically. It doesn't happen very often any more, but when it does it's another reminder of how not-perfect I am.' It's a comparison that, conscious or not, a lot of us are making. In 2022, health researchers in Spain conducted a review of existing research on pornography's relationship to body dissatisfaction and found compelling evidence that the more porn you see, the worse you feel about your body.[2] Across twenty-six studies, only three found no association between porn exposure and negative body image and – despite the fact that men who watch porn are regularly confronted with penises that are bigger, thicker and harder for longer than their own – the impact on body image was most pronounced for heterosexual women about one body part in particular: their vulva.

Amelia grew up in a white Irish Catholic family with parents who, perhaps contrary to expectation, would talk to her regularly about sex and made sure she didn't have a sense that it was morally wrong. They would answer her questions honestly and carefully and it meant she became something of an oracle to the other kids at school. 'I've been having conversations about things like vibrators since I was about fourteen,' she said. 'My friends used to think I knew more than they did about the subject, so they would come to me and would say, "I've just done this, is that normal?" I never had any problem talking about it.'

Amelia said she stumbled across porn online at

eleven or twelve. It was back in the day when pop-ups were ubiquitous on the internet and browsers hadn't yet developed in-built mechanisms to block them. She was shocked at first but curious, and started clicking through trying to access the content. Looking back, she thinks she was a bit obsessed; regularly trying to get onto the sites, thinking she'd learn the stuff about sex that her parents wouldn't tell her. With the tenacity of a pre-teen, she eventually managed to do it, bypassing a paywall and finding her way through to something much more graphic. She can't remember exactly what she saw but she definitely remembers the feeling. 'I felt gross,' she said, 'but it wasn't about the images. I felt gross that it turned me on. It was a really icky feeling, and from then on I decided that I wasn't going to do it any more.'

For the next few years, Amelia was largely able to follow through on her decision, until she moved in with her partner. His sister mentioned to her that he had a stash of porn magazines under his bed at his parents' house. She was curious to know what he was looking at so she asked him and he showed her, but like getting past the paywall, she wasn't ready for what she would see. It turned out that the entire surface area underneath his childhood bed was full of boxes and boxes and boxes of porn magazines that he'd collected over the years. Instead of arousal this time, Amelia felt insecure. 'I was with him at the time and I remember looking at the magazines and looking at him thinking, "Oh, I don't look like that, is that what he finds attractive?" It wasn't good for my self-esteem,' she said. Like Luce, it was one part of the body in particular that was really giving her that feeling. Not the breasts or butt that we might expect – Amelia was judging her vulva. 'A lot of the vaginas in the magazines all looked exactly the same and looked nothing like mine. With so little exposure to naked images and naked people as we grow up, all we know is what ours looks like,' she said. 'Then we see pictures of ones that have probably had some kind of surgery, and you measure yourself up against that. It means you're always going to fall short, especially if it's not real.' Amelia and her boyfriend were together for twelve years after that and her feeling of bodily insecurity eventually passed. But Isobel had noticed a similar impact for a lot of younger women in her role as a doctor in general practice.

Isobel was close to forty now and had started using porn in the last couple of years. Though she watched it she said she felt fairly ambivalent, and was concerned about the impact it had on her and other people. 'I have a lot of reservations generally about the pornography industry, about people being exploited, people's health and safety. I also have some concerns about whether mainstream porn gives people an idea of sex as something that men do to women,' she told me. 'And then there's the impact it's having on bodies and what people expect to be normal and achievable. I don't want to be judging people who have had cosmetic surgery but most people's bodies don't look like they do in porn.'

Isobel said she'd been worried about the number of women coming into her practice thinking there was something wrong with their vulva. However, it wasn't only because they had seen other vulvas in porn; it was more about what porn had meant for them seeing their own. 'Nobody has any pubic hair any more,' she said. 'I talked about that with one of my friends who is a doctor as well. When we first started training twenty years ago most people had pubic hair, and now pretty much everybody under forty is waxed completely. I think porn starts to impact on people even if they are not people who necessarily directly use it. If there is a general awareness of what images are out there and what other people's expectations are, the impact of it spreads.' She didn't care about the hair itself; after all, what you do with the hair on your body is entirely up to you. But it was affecting her work and what patients presented with, because it revealed their vulvas to them, often for the first time. And that seemed to be taking quite a few of them aback. 'It's people thinking that their genitals don't look right,' she told me. '"My labia are too big." We hear that now fairly often. I say, "Yes. That's because when you had a load of pubic hair you couldn't really see them. Now you are looking at them and of course they look more prominent because you haven't got anything else down there."'

A former nurse who now worked as a sexual health and pleasure expert, Sam talked about the same thing. 'The problem,' she told me, 'is that now we've ripped all the hair off we can see each other's vaginas and labia. We never saw them before and no one actually realized that they all were really very different.' She talked about the importance of seeing other women's vulvas, not to compare to your own but just to know how different we all are. Things like Jamie McCartney's *Great Wall of Vulva*, a nine-metre-long sculpted artwork consisting of 400 plaster casts of vulvas – it's online if you'd like to see it. Sam knew a gynaecologist who kept McCartney's coffee-table book on his desk and used it with the young women increasingly coming in and saying they thought there was something wrong with their external genitalia. He'd open it up and ask which one looked like theirs. They'd realize all vulvas look different. And that'd be the end of that. 'What is shocking,' Sam said, 'is that he is having teenagers coming in at all. This is on the NHS, it's a waste of money. I've got women who can't even get seen for their endometriosis symptoms. Why are young girls being referred for this?'

Almost fifty years ago the shaming of the female body and what it means for our reluctance to get to know ourselves better was tackled by a group of women in Boston, Massachusetts, by publishing the first edition of *Our Bodies, Ourselves*, a book that stayed in print until 2018. It was a revolutionary first; originally a stapled pamphlet, the text included accurate diagrams and information about the female body, speaking directly and frankly to women about everything from anatomy to sexual health and menopause. The format was so useful, in fact, that it was adapted in 2014, with *Trans Bodies, Trans Selves* taking a similar stand, written by and for the transgender community. *Our Bodies,*

Ourselves advocated something called 'vaginal self-examination', encouraging women to look at themselves in a mirror while they were reading the diagrams explaining what was where. It was a practice that was popular in feminist self-help groups in the seventies and one that Gwyneth Paltrow tried to revive with her 2020 Netflix show, *The Goop Lab*.

In one episode titled 'The Pleasure is Ours' Paltrow gave viewers a front-row seat as the then ninety-year-old Betty Dodson – an American sex educator who has been helping women with orgasms since the seventies – talked through the process of self-examination. She explained the importance of seeing not just your own vulva but also other women's, so that, like McCartney's wall, we see how different we all are. But before we start thinking of Paltrow as an advocate for a modern feminist approach to sexual health education, she has also extolled the benefits of vaginal steaming, something that Sam told me was definitely not in the vagina's best interests. Anyway, maybe these days we don't need self-help groups to see vulvas, our own or anyone else's. It was here that Hester saw a role for porn.

Hester was a thirty-six-year-old white woman who had two kids in her mid-twenties. She was also bisexual and married to a straight man, which gave porn a particular purpose. 'I think for me porn is about meeting the needs or interests that aren't met in my actual relationship. Not filling a gap exactly but it's the bits of me I don't get to express day-to-day,' she said. 'I am much more interested in queer porn, not in watching straight people have sex. I find the mainstream stuff quite violent and gross. I can't speak for all women, but I don't want to see some girl with guys coming all over her face.'

It meant that Hester mostly sought out porn that wasn't on mainstream sites. She had a subscription for a while to SuicideGirls, which features 'alternative women' (think piercings and tattoos). And when we talked, she was using CrashPad – the site Leonora had tried for a while – which advertises itself as showing real queer sex that real queer people want to have on camera. It also meant she was critical of the porn debate more broadly, and what it meant for how we thought about women and their relationship to sex. 'The way most of the mainstream policy debate around porn is framed gives women no agency, we're just passive victims,' she told me. 'Whether that is people producing porn or people as consumers, there seems to be no acknowledgement of women as sexual beings ourselves, not just people that bad things happen to done by bad men. If you say, "Porn is just terrible. It's disastrous and ruining our youth" then that takes away our ability to talk about it. The reality is that loads of people, I would guess the majority, have some experience with porn. The debate is too often framed as only the deviant people do this. That way of seeing it stops you having a sensible conversation with young people.'

Partly because she'd looked for this range in porn, Hester had had a different experience with what it meant for her body. She said she'd found it positive to see bodies like hers, ones that aren't perfect and don't conform to that picture of how our bodies should be. And she also thought that this was missing from the public conversation; the possibility that porn could play a part in helping women understand that actually there's no such thing as normal. 'One of the things that really bugs me,' she said, 'is all the hand-wringing about people getting unrealistic expectations from porn about what genitalia should look like, about body hair, the idea of perfect vaginas and the pressure that puts young girls under. That might be true to an extent but the fact is that most girls have not seen anyone else's vagina. So, seeing some on the internet is more useful than not seeing any; it helps normalize human bodies.' She still thought it could be better. I don't want to see loads of fake tits,' she said. 'But it's better than not seeing any and thinking you're the only person who looks like you do. It might be flawed but at least it's something.' In a context where we can barely say the word 'vulva', it might be that she's right.

Touching ourselves

There is a scene in *Black Swan*, the 2010 film that scored a Best Actress Oscar for Natalie Portman, where Portman's character masturbates in the bath and is almost caught by her mother. The scene is slow, erotic and incredibly graphic, so much so that it caused waves when it came out, especially given how rarely female masturbation is shown on the big screen. Portman later described the scene as 'so disgusting', which pretty much sums up the problem.[3] If there's been something unspeakable about certain parts of the female body, there's an even bigger taboo about the fact that, sometimes, we might want to touch them. And it's particularly pronounced when applied to women. There's a range of terms for male masturbation – 'wanking', 'jerking', 'spanking the monkey' and so on – and numerous Hollywood films where men's masturbatory practices unashamedly take centre-stage. Those of us of a certain generation will remember the movie *American Pie*, when the unlikely hero is caught masturbating into baked goods. It was definitely a talking point when the movie came out, but I'm not sure it was referred to as disgusting.

Things are a little better for women on the small screen, which these days isn't quite so small. HBO's *Sex and the City* is often regarded as one of the first shows to really be open about the fact that women might get ourselves off, but these days shows like Netflix's *Sex Education* and *Dear White People* or the BBC's *Fleabag* have picked up the baton and run with it, going places where *Sex and the City* didn't. This greater representation might have something to do with the mainstreaming of porn, because as our access has increased so too has it become harder to dismiss masturbation as only for men. In many ways that's a good thing; porn is not only used to masturbate but it is a big part of its purpose, and so on one level the mainstreaming of porn has implicitly brought with it an acknowledgement that masturbation isn't weird or shameful, it's just a part of our sexual lives. It's a message that many of the women I spoke to didn't get growing up.

Anita was in her twenties when we spoke, the daughter of parents who emigrated to the UK from India, and someone who these days spoke openly and honestly about sex to anyone who would listen. She said that when she was younger no one talked about the fact that women might want sex. She saw a sexual double standard running through her family, not directly from her parents but from uncles, aunties and grandparents. An uncle once said to his son, her seventeen-year-old cousin, that he could mess about with any woman he wanted – 'white ones, whatever' – but he should bring home a brown woman who's a virgin. It was something she's since told her mum about and they've spoken together about how messed up it is. But it wasn't just from home that she was getting the message that sex and sexuality isn't for girls.

'I remember in secondary school,' she told me, 'my friends and I wouldn't talk about porn or masturbation. It was like, "Ugh, so-and-so says she fingers herself." There was this rumour about one girl and the showerhead in sixth form and we were all just like, "Oh my God, that's so disgusting."' What she learned from home was reinforced; if sex isn't for girls, then masturbation isn't either. But girls are curious and Anita was interested so a few months later in the shower she gave it a go. 'I was blown away, like "This is amazing," and I wished I had the courage to tell all of my female friends to do it,' she said. 'Even with your friends that you were closest to, you were always testing each other. I can remember looks between us where someone actually wanted to share that this is something they do, but it was such a forbidden thing for us to talk about. The boys, though; boys, they come out of the womb masturbating, don't they? They're like, "Yeah, I'm a proper bloke, I masturbate."'

It was similar for Elizabeth, a white woman who was in her mid-thirties and grew up in a house where the topic of sex was off the table – even if it came up on TV, she said her parents would change the channel. It meant that as a teenager she didn't know much about what went on between people in the bedroom, and even less about the sexual pleasure that we can give ourselves. Which made it even more surprising when one day, almost accidentally, she made herself come. 'I remember being sixteen the first time that I made myself orgasm, and I didn't know what was going on,' she told me, laughing. 'I was just playing around and seeing what happened. I remember very clearly thinking, "There must be something wrong."' She said that even though it felt nice, she knew it wasn't something to discuss. There was something immediately shameful about it, a feeling that was confirmed by the other girls in school. 'I remember it was brought up once by another girl,' she said. 'And one of my friends turned to me and was like, "Well, I don't know how she does it, because it's not a nice thing to do, is it?" And I just kind of agreed. I was very aware of the fact that I wasn't to talk about it.'

It seems that girls can talk about anything, as long as it's not that we touch ourselves. It's made worse by the way our masturbation is represented, that is when it's represented at all. Like porn for women, women's masturbation is usually seen as something softer than men's. It's sensual and romantic, it takes time and effort. But as Rowan showed getting off in her GCSEs, the realities can be – well – mundane. 'I can remember masturbating as a teenager in Antigua,' Louisa told me. 'And I wanted something to focus on that didn't carry any shame. So, I'd masturbate looking at home decorating magazines.

Not because they were arousing, just because they'd help me concentrate.' This sense of masturbation as not necessarily something sexual carried over into how Louisa felt about it when we spoke. She was nearing forty and had been single for a while and told me what she did was more perfunctory than anything else. 'I know when I read about people's masturbation habits it seems very celebratory, they have these amazing orgasms,' she said. 'But I've always thought of it as being something quite functional, like you would sneeze because you need to, or cough to get rid of a frog in your throat.' For Vanessa it was the same. She was in her late twenties and told me that the way she got herself off was far from the silk negligees you see on *Sex and the City*. 'Masturbation for me is very boring. It's like a day-in, day-out thing,' she said. 'I do it because I'm tired or bored or stressed. Or maybe my vagina is uncomfortable; it's itchy or dry. I masturbate to sort it out. It's very humdrum.'

The original seventies pamphlet that became *Our Bodies, Ourselves* didn't only try to break the silence about looking at our vulvas, it also tried to address some of the mythology about how and why women masturbate. It talked about some women masturbating by rubbing their clitoris or inserting fingers and objects, but also by squeezing their legs together, using pillows or running water. And it also addressed the reasons we do it, which sometimes are far from sexual. The core message was about finding out what your body likes – not feeling constrained by the choices of others – and feeling OK with what you do, and what you don't. Even as adult women, it's something we still don't hear enough. And, sadly, it looks like most porn isn't helping to shake the feeling that there's one 'right' way to do it.

Kathy started masturbating around twelve, not often, just every few months. She created a whole ritual which was well thought-out for a pre-teen. First, she'd make a hot chocolate and tell her mum she was having time to herself, then she'd go into her room and put some music on, lie on her bed and look up at her walls. 'There was a singer called D'Angelo,' she said, 'and I had this poster where he was almost naked. I had lots of other ones, like Lil' Bow Wow and stuff. They helped me set the mood.' Kathy's father was a Pentecostal Christian and it meant that, like in Anita's family, female sexuality was kept quiet – she remembers getting in trouble with an aunt once for even saying the word 'boyfriend'. So, after a couple of years of her having 'time to herself' she thinks her dad clocked on to what it was all about. When she was fifteen one day she walked into her room and all the posters were gone. No one ever mentioned it.

Kathy was in her late twenties and ran her own dance studio when I interviewed her. She had a real openness about her; I felt a deep sense of confidence in the way she spoke that only comes from a real acceptance of yourself. She'd been using porn on and off since being introduced to Pornhub by her boyfriend at eighteen, but that sense of acceptance hadn't always extended to masturbation: up until a year ago she thought she was strange because she kept it all external. 'I have this weird thing about masturbating. I could never insert anything into myself,' she told me. 'I don't even wear tampons. I just can't do it. I'm a grown woman, I've had a baby, and I don't even insert a finger.' She said her friends thought she had some mental barriers and had bought her a vibrator to help. But she couldn't do it, she just didn't want to. 'I've half tried,' she said, 'but honestly, it's just too much effort.' It had taken most of her life so far but Kathy finally didn't think what she did – or didn't do – was strange. She told me she felt OK with it now, that it worked for her and that was enough. But I did still get the sense that she thought she was an outlier, and it was the same sense I got from Almina.

At twenty now, Almina grew up with the internet, which meant she didn't need posters on her wall for inspiration, but when I asked her if she masturbated, she told me that she didn't. She'd orgasmed to the porn she'd been watching since her early teens – she just wasn't sure if that counted. 'I remember when I was in sixth form the guys were talking about masturbation,' she told me. 'They looked at me and said, "Don't you masturbate?" and I said, "No." To this day I'm not sure whether me just watching porn and orgasming is masturbating. In my head masturbating is me inserting something in my vagina but I've never actually fingered myself.'

That both Kathy and Almina thought what they did was unusual says something about the differences between what we're told about women's masturbation and what most of us actually do. Because when you turn to the research on women's self-pleasuring practices, it looks like a lot of women are doing the same thing as them.

Alfred Kinsey's famous sexuality study published in 1953 was probably the first to debunk the idea that most women penetrate themselves in some way when they masturbate. Kinsey found that just over 80 per cent of the close to 3,000

American women interviewed didn't insert anything vaginally when they masturbated. A little over twenty years later, the feminist sex educator Shere Hite conducted a similar study focused solely on women. Again, she found, with a sample of almost 2,000 American women, that penetration during masturbation wasn't that common; roughly 90 per cent of women said that they didn't regularly do it. Despite this, a study in 2014 found that most women assumed that other women did penetrate themselves during masturbation, even though they didn't do it themselves.[4] It's an assumption that is reproduced regularly in a lot of porn where women are shown penetrating themselves – and each other – almost every time they get the chance. It's not hard to work out why this is; after all, if we do away with the idea that women always need penetration for pleasure then that's a serious blow for heterosexual men. What's missing is the sense that we can define for ourselves how and when, where and why we touch our own bodies. Maybe like Hester's point about porn helping to normalize our vulvas, porn could have a role here. Isabella certainly thought so.

Like Almina, Isabella had grown up with the internet and had been watching porn regularly since her late teens. At twenty-four when we spoke, she told me that for her generation porn was a major part of culture. It was something she'd talked about with friends, though with some she knew not to mention it. 'When I was younger, I think I was fifteen or sixteen, I was talking with two friends of mine about masturbation,' she said. 'One of my friends, even though she had had sex with men, she had never masturbated. The other one had masturbated but she found it a bit disgusting when I mentioned I touch myself directly as she had only masturbated by touching her pants. So, the fact that she felt disgusted by that gave me the information that I can't really talk to her about my usage of porn. Because I also find that many women tend to talk about porn as if it's disgusting, whereas for me it's been quite useful.'

Isabella was realistic; she didn't think that all porn on all sites was great. But while she was concerned about some of what she'd seen, overall she thought her experience of porn was mostly a positive one. 'Through using porn, I masturbated quite a lot. In a way it shaped my preferences, but it also taught me how I like to be touched,' she said. 'It allowed me to get in touch with my body and be sexual with myself before I had any sexual intercourse with anyone else. For me, that was important because when I started having sex with other people, I felt that I knew what I liked and what I didn't. I knew what I wanted, I knew how to have orgasms, I knew where and when I wanted things to stop.' Porn didn't just help Isabella touch herself, it helped her know and ask for what she wanted. She used it to learn that she wasn't just there for somebody else; that her body, and pleasure, were hers.

Seeing ourselves

When George Floyd, a forty-six-year-old African-American man, was killed in Minnesota by a white police officer in May 2020, it sparked worldwide protests – both in the streets and online. Marches were held in over 2,000 cities globally and 'Blackout Tuesday' was organized by the music industry to show solidarity with the movements against racism and police brutality. Organizations and individuals were encouraged to post a black square on their social media for the day, and Pornhub quickly got in on the act, tweeting that 'Pornhub stands in solidarity against racism and social injustice' and pledging $100,000 to organizations actively fighting for equality.[5]

The post received a lot of attention but perhaps not in the way the company had expected. Campaigning groups and individuals started to point out that, far from being anti-racist, Pornhub actually had a race problem. A range of videos and titles from the site were posted as evidence, including those describing Black men being dominated by white police officers or the Ku Klux Klan, and a video of a white female porn actress wearing a 'White Lives Matter' T-shirt and using the N-word to say that Black lives do not. Pornhub was quick to respond with its corporate line that the hosting of what it termed 'race play' on the platform was a consensual adult kink and as such should be respected. The fact that it was able to make these two simultaneous statements, on the one hand fighting for racial equality while on the other profiting from the fact that some, let's face it mostly white, people want to masturbate to racist representations shows just how little we talk about race, and racism, in pornography. It's something that the British journalist and author Yomi Adegoke wrote about in 2019, stating that 'a need to appear liberal and open-minded has left many modern feminists uncharacteristically quiet' about porn and race. And she's right. Most of the women I spoke to who were white, like myself, would recognize some level of racism in porn but were able to keep a distance. Seeing ourselves was all about gender; whiteness was rarely acknowledged. But for women of colour it was different: there was another part of the equation. Because our bodies aren't just about how porn sees women, they're also about how porn sees race.

It wasn't just her masturbation that had left Almina feeling like the odd one out. She thought that young women were stuck between two conflicting forces: society saying porn wasn't for girls and the boys who kept wanting them to watch it. So after first having porn used as a form of harassment by the boys, messaging her with links and pictures in her early teens, she started to look for it herself. 'Most porn is about being sexual for men. It is all about the man pleasing himself. It made it feel like porn is something I wasn't supposed to be watching. There is this red flag that says, "Don't watch it or talk about it." I even have that when I am discussing it with you right now,' she told me. 'At the same time, boys who want to sexually arouse you are sending it over. Everyone else is saying, "Don't go near it," and then they are saying, "Go near it for me." I was just interested in what was going on. I just wanted to see what sex looked like, what their bodies looked like and what they were doing.'

This desire to use porn to understand not just sex but bodies created a real problem. Because Almina was Black and all the bodies she saw were white. 'For the longest time I thought there was something wrong with me; that my body wasn't normal because of what I saw in porn,' she told me. 'Most porn mainly shows white women. I wasn't watching porn with Black women in it when I was growing up and developing. Right now, I have stretch marks and I have strawberry legs where my hair follicles look like black holes, my knees are darker than the rest of my legs, my butt is a different colour and my arms too so there is discoloration all over my body. Even my vulva area is darker than the rest of my body and when you watch porn their entire body is one colour and looks perfect. There are no blemishes or hair. I thought there was clearly something wrong with me because my body does not look like theirs.'

Through porn Almina had access to an endless gallery of women, all of whom had the same single skin colour. It made her feel even more different, particularly given the prevailing silence around the female body. That infinite supermarket stood in for the whole story and it meant that as a teenager she really struggled with her self-esteem. 'No one clarifies what your body is supposed to look like,' she told me, 'or what it does or what sex is. And then you see that a video has ten million views and you think that if it has that many, that body must be desirable and that must be what sex should look like. Everyone says it's not reality but that doesn't sink in because there's nothing else to compare it to.'

It took a while but when I met her, Almina was getting closer to self-acceptance. She'd started having sex and realized that her partners didn't care if her butt was darker than her legs, which helped her to stop caring too, or at least to not care as much. She'd also started watching porn that had more Black women in it. She said seeing herself represented helped, but for other racially minoritized women that was exactly what they tried to avoid.

Simone was a photographer in her early twenties, and an advocate for Black British women like herself. She felt that the silence around women's use of pornography was an extension of the sanction on women's sexuality in general. 'I think the lack of wanting or feeling like we're able to talk about porn comes from not only women but also from men,' she said. 'And when we do talk about porn or women and sex, women's pleasure is always discussed in relationship to the pleasure of men. We're not able to be agents of sexual desire ourselves.' She'd started watching porn sparingly over the last two years, after asking a long-term boyfriend if he would show her what to look for. She said she always used to think of it as quite a seedy thing, and though that's changed the more that she's seen, there's still a feeling of conflict. 'Over time I've become less offended by things. I think there's definitely an element of violence which I still find quite uncomfortable,' she said. 'I look at things which are more girl-on-girl focused and I think most of my friends are like that. But I still go through pangs of guilt when I do. I rush down the list and watch something and still sometimes it's just sad. I feel like I read too much into it so I can't enjoy it any more.'

One of the main problems for Simone was the representation of Black women and what that meant for how she felt she was perceived. 'I like the idea of seeing myself reflected in the media and things that I digest,' she said. 'So, I have actively searched for things which have people that look like me in it. But normally that's more traumatic than anything else – it's all Big Black this, you know, everything is fetishized. It makes me feel ill.' Simone thought it was symptomatic of wider culture, built on years and years of Black and minoritized people being 'othered'. So, though it isn't porn's fault that people who look like her are fetishized, she felt it contributed to a culture where racist stereotypes keep getting reproduced. Given the amount of mainstream porn people watch, that poses a real barrier to changing a racist culture.

All of this meant that unlike the use that Almina found in watching porn of Black women, Simone, who was usually a strong supporter of Black media, said she wouldn't encourage racialized people to look for themselves in porn. 'I wouldn't recommend Black people actively seek representations of themselves in that type of media because we are seen as this other, this hypersexual being. I've not pursued it again myself. It's like, no, put it back in the cupboard.'

Anita, who was blown away by the showerhead as a teenager, also told me that the way porn showed women like her was racist, and so she tried to find her way around it, with varying degrees of success. 'I'm a South Asian woman,

I'm Indian, so for me it just feels so cringey when I see these categories all about race,' she said. 'It feeds all these nasty racist stereotypes that we already have in society and just sits really uncomfortably with me. I only watch girl-on-girl and I've tried to find videos where it was two South Asian women so that I can see myself reflected, but I either haven't been able to find that many videos like that or when I have found them, they've been done so badly that actually I would just prefer to watch white women.' Anita had attempted to stop watching porn altogether but it didn't really work. She felt her ability to fantasize without it had been compromised and ultimately – even with its faults – it worked as a kind of quick fix. 'To a certain extent we get conditioned; if I want to get off, porn is just easier,' she said. 'I would say it's harder for me to use my imagination now, I just don't come that quickly. So, I try and negotiate it as best as I can, but I still feel like I get a bit lazy. To be honest I should probably just watch less porn, but instead I try to find the least offensive video possible.'

Vanessa, who'd spoken about masturbation as an everyday 'humdrum' thing, had a slightly different take on it all. She'd grown up in the nineties with top-shelf porn magazines which, though she could never reach them, she'd always found intriguing. It meant that when, at fifteen, her family got Freeview and she found out about the free samplers on the pay-for-porn channels, she started watching them almost nightly. It was the same thing every evening, five to ten minutes of softcore porn, women on beds pretending to talk on the phone, but she didn't mind the repetition. At eighteen she moved away for university, got time alone and her own computer. And she started watching porn that she searched for herself which turned out to be quite different from those samplers on TV. 'I can't speak for anyone else, but often I am aware that what I find sexy or arousing in pornography are the storylines and the stuff that is around it. For me, there's loads of fucked-up stuff in what I watch about gender and power and age,' she said. 'I think despite having read a fuck ton of theory and saying all the right things, that stuff is deeply rooted in my psyche. Deeply rooted in what sex is to me. So, I watch quite a lot of porn about intergenerational dynamics – like here's this guy fucking his step-daughter. Or this guy sleeping with his daughter's friend. Then there's another box of weird stuff about rapes. Interracial stuff too which I find really problematic.' There was something in this last category in particular that gave Vanessa a similar feeling to Almina. It wasn't without its complications but as a Black woman it was a way of seeing Black women being celebrated.

'The stuff which is Black women and white men, what I like is seeing white men lose their shit,' she told me. 'Like there is one pornography performer in particular. In some ways it's really fetishizing, but he kisses Black women loads and is obsessed with their bums. He is really into them and kind of worships them. And I watch it for ages. Like I watch it and watch it and hold myself back from orgasming just because I don't see that very often. And the stuff with Black men and white women is so hinged on this idea of the Black man as a buck and aggressive and violent. But imagining myself as this white woman being fucked in that way, occupying this really held-up, worshipped vision of femininity that white women hold, that women of colour don't have access to, which I'm critical of, and challenge. It is really problematic but I watch it.'

As Vanessa's searches included interracial porn together with various themes of violence, the site's algorithms would send more of that to her. It meant that she'd had vidoes come up that she's found really disturbing and they speak to the racism in porn. 'In the periphery of what I'm watching there is all of this really fucked-up stuff, full of real hate and aggression. Like "Black bitch is fucked by KKK", or "made to choke on a confederate flag". Or white women police officers fucking Black men. It upsets me to think about the experience of the men making that.'

Vanessa was open and honest when we spoke in a way that I think surprised us both. She was working things out for herself as we were talking, and it meant she had a realization there was one kind of porn that she didn't watch, ever. 'I never watch pornography that is two Black people having sex, you know, and I am not quite sure why that is. I can remember having a really drunk conversation with some other Black women who also said the same. I wonder if there is a part of me that still holds love between two Black people as something sacred. Maybe love between two Black people holds an intimacy that is precious to me – that I don't want porn to spoil. So, what's going on with the rest of the porn that I watch?' she asked without wanting an answer. 'There is a part of me that wants to say I'm at peace with what turns me on. But that's not true. I'm not. It's fucked up. There's stuff happening there for me that I should deal with at some point. And I will at some point. But not today.'

It might seem obvious to say it, but porn is about our bodies – in more ways than one. There's porn about women with big bodies, petite bodies. Porn where we're just described by our skin or hair colour, whole categories devoted to the size of our breasts. So, what does that mean when it's women who're watching? On the one hand, porn can help us learn about ourselves; using the range of bodies we see as a way to make sense of, and accept, our own. But on the other, we're in a world that judges our bodies based on gender and race. And porn's not just produced – and used – in that world; for many of us it feels like it feeds it.

SEX

The promise of positivity

WHETHER OR NOT WE USE it, porn means something for sex. It can give us and our partners inspiration and instruction; it can be used as a form of education in both useful and less useful ways. It can help us explore what we like and what we don't, and can give men expectations they put on us to fulfil. It means that conversations with women about porn inevitably include what goes on in the bedroom. And there, across different perspectives, the same experience appears: the struggle women have to get to a place where sex feels like it's actually for us.

When you look around it's hard to avoid the number of articles framing sex as a problem for women. While *Cosmopolitan* explains the '8 reasons you're not orgasming', *Glamour* declares,

'No libido, no problem. Here's how to increase your sex drive'.[1] In fact, type 'Why women don't . . .' into Google and the first suggestion is likely to be why women don't want sex. We're supposed to agree to sex or refuse it, consent perhaps but never initiate. Paris Hilton summed it up best: 'I may be sexy but I'm not a very sexual person.'[2] It's an image of women that's challenged by the sex positive focus on pleasure. But it's also an image that some of us hold onto, and Victoria had some ideas about why and what it meant for porn.

Victoria was a white Irish woman in her mid-forties with an unabashed honesty and a mouth like a sailor. 'Women need to get their finger out and start being a bit more honest about the fact that they're human,' she told me. 'There's this sense of fuck it, we've got nothing else so let's cling to this idea of being morally superior. It's a way to hold onto power when we don't have very much in other aspects of our lives, but actually it's not helpful. It's a prison that involves waxing and no underarm hair and polite sex. It's a prison that would have us celebrate our impotence, you know, "We're moral, we're wonderful, we have no pleasure and thank God for the fucking menopause." Really?! Jesus! Have we lost our minds?'

Victoria watched porn, sometimes a lot of it, and she'd reflected a fair bit over the years about why so many women don't. She felt that the way women are told we should feel about porn was the same as how we should feel about sex; we should find it disgusting or exploitative, not enjoyable, we should feel threatened instead of aroused. And she thought that this was because holding down our sexual needs gives us a much-needed sense of superiority. We're told we're intellectually inferior and physically inferior, so projecting a sense that we're morally superior – that we don't like sex and that makes us better than men – can feel pretty inviting. It was something she'd had to work hard to overcome.

'The turning point for me in my life, and I'm about to be very graphic, was the lover I was with for a decade when I was in my mid-twenties,' she said. 'Very early in the piece I got on top of him and I turned round to him and I said, "Do you mind if I just use you?" and he said, "No, not at all," and I took myself off to a degree that I had never, ever experienced before. I remember thinking, "Fuck me, that's how this is supposed to go," and he was absolutely delighted. I was in a trajectory in my own head anyway and I think one way or the other things would have worked out, but every single woman should be told, "Stick him down on the ground and use the equipment how you will." Because that is what every man is told. Men are told their pleasure is automatic and women are saturated with media about how difficult it is for us to orgasm. We're told from day one that our pleasure is abnormal, that sex is great but you're probably not going to get the best out of it, just prepare yourself for that and you'll be OK.' When she lays it out like that, it's no wonder so many of us haven't had the best time in the bedroom.

In contrast to the relatively few academic studies on women's use of porn, there's a research interest bordering on obsession with how much women do, or more accurately do not, want to have sex. For most of the twentieth century this focus was on frigidity, described by the writer Bea Campbell as 'the diagnosis offered by men to the women they'd failed to "satisfy" or rather women who'd failed to be satisfied'.[3] The point about the failure being ours is important.

In the forties it was estimated that close to 80 per cent of women were frigid, with two main theories offered as to why this was. The first was clinical; that frigidity was an illness, the result of women's innate neuroses, and needed to be treated with physical and psychological therapy (it's no surprise that the origin of the word 'hysteria' is the ancient Greek word for 'uterus'). The second was that it wasn't really a problem at all, rather it was right for the right kind of woman not to feel sexual pleasure, to reject everything sexual as indecent, and to submit to sex with reluctance. While the clinical explanation seems to have fallen mostly by the wayside, you just need to hear what women have been told about sex to see the respectability one is still going strong.

When we spoke, Jade was in her late thirties and had led what many would say was a fairly conventional life. She grew up, like a lot of women I know, in a white Christian household with parents that probably should have divorced and a deafening silence when it came to sex. When she first came across pornography, she was somewhere between ten and twelve; initially it was a magazine her dad had and pretty soon after that she found one of her mum's. She didn't talk to them about it, didn't ask any questions, just felt pretty confused by what she had seen. Up until that point all she knew about sex was that it was something you did in the context of a loving relationship, but the pictures she saw in the magazines weren't showing that and she wasn't sure what to make of it. She put it to one side and didn't see porn again, or think at all about sex really, until she started having it herself in her late teens.

Jade told me she wasn't ready when she first had sex, she wasn't comfortable with herself or her body. It was just that she felt like she should, not that there was any real desire. 'People had sex with me when I was younger, never the other way around,' she said. 'It would be like, "Oh, well, I've been going out with you for a while, I should really." Not like there was anyone I desperately wanted.' She connected this to how little she knew about sex and how what she did know was that it wasn't for her. She'd always thought sex was a little bit weird, not something women would really want unless they were the wrong kind of woman. 'When you're young you're not given ownership of it,' she said. 'You're not told, "This is a perfectly normal feeling, enjoy it, accept it." You're seen as too forward if you're the driving force but then you're seen as the gatekeeper if you don't want to. It's only as you get to your thirties or forties that you think actually, "No, this is mine as well."'

I heard a similar story from many of the women that I spoke to. It seems to take years before our sex feels like ours. For some women, like Kate, porn played a big part in getting there.

Growing up in Northern Ireland in the seventies, Kate was told explicitly that sex was not for women. 'I remember my mother would put her fingers into a circle the size of a ten pence piece. And then she'd make a fist and say, "Sex is like trying to put a fist into that, so don't do it."' Kate said she was told that sex was for your husband, that it was about pleasing them. 'And if we get any pleasure out of it, oh fair enough. But that's by the by. It's not actually for us.' It had meant that she'd felt she couldn't talk about sex for years and didn't really explore what she wanted until she was much older. When she did, she found what she wanted was to be sexually submissive. 'When I was younger the internet didn't exist,' she said. 'I didn't get online until my twenties. When I started accessing porn it was by myself, not with my partner. And I found gay male porn a real turn on and then I got into BDSM, which is what I use now.' Kate had been with her partner since her late teens and said that while their relationship was good, their sex life wasn't great. It meant that she'd used porn to carve out a space where she could explore a part of her sexuality. And then she took those explorations offline. 'I've been with my partner for a long time and sexually it's not fulfilling any more,' she said. 'Looking back, I didn't always see myself as being a submissive but I was always very sexual, always interested in sex. So now I look for BDSM relationships to satisfy that need.'

Though Kate didn't talk to her long-term partner about it, she told me she'd worked hard on herself to get to the place she was at. A place where she felt OK in herself to say what felt good and accept what it was that she wanted. She didn't think society helped women to get there. 'I'm quite happy talking about what I need and what I watch but I know a lot of women feel really uncomfortable about that. I think women should be encouraged more to speak about it. It is a natural part of who we are, our bodies are created to enjoy sex,' she said. 'But we lie to ourselves, we aren't totally honest with ourselves and I don't know why that is. Even my long-term partner doesn't know the other part of my sexuality. I feel uncomfortable with him sometimes. I'm not sure if that's a fear of opening myself up. We just need to get rid of that whole taboo that sex is dirty somehow. Sure, it's something that goes on behind closed doors but sex is an extremely pleasurable experience.'

The feeling that sex wasn't for women was enough for Jade and Kate to have spent large parts of their sexual lives unfulfilled but unable to say it. They both told me they hoped it was different for the next generation, but despite growing up in the age of information, surrounded by female role models reclaiming and celebrating sex, women decades younger than them spoke in similar terms. Like Louise in her early twenties, who told me that if she'd had a one-night stand with a man and was feeling good about it, when she told her friends there'd still be an underlying judgement. Or Frances, who was the same age and had the same experience, saying that the dichotomy of slut or prude dominated attitudes towards sex at her school. But there were also some younger women using porn as a way of pushing back; a way of rejecting the stigma about women and sex, and Abigail was one of them.

At twenty-two, Abigail had already been using porn for close to ten years after finding stories about BDSM on a young writers' forum at thirteen. She felt porn helped her understand her own sexuality without the shame that is a part of so many women's experiences, and told me that was a benefit of porn; that it can open up society to understanding the range and breadth of sex. 'It can promote an understanding that sexual desires are not necessarily a monolith, that people have different fantasies, different desires and wants and needs,' she told me. 'Porn is a vehicle that can justify your fantasies and not make people feel so ashamed of what it is that they want.' She felt that porn can lead to people being more open and comfortable with their sexuality, that it is one of those few things that can elicit that reassurance: what you like might be a little bit weird but it's also OK to like it. It was a view that Beth, at twenty-eight, shared. 'It's helped me to be more open about sexuality and sex, to have a dialogue, even if it's just with myself, like, "Why don't I like that? Maybe I want to watch this,"' she said. 'Because I still think that being openly sexual as a woman is spoken about in derogatory terms. You know, "the slut", "you're a slag", and "whore", and all the rest of it. But porn helps us have at least a sexual conversation with ourselves, becoming aroused on our own, and not for the purpose of having sex, or for the purpose of anyone else.' She's right about this function of porn, and it's one of the only things that can do that. But it also made me wonder what all of that means when we add in how porn has been implicated in reproducing the negative picture about openly sexual women.

A recent study found worrying parallels between the language on mainstream porn sites and that used by 'Incels' – a mostly online community of men who incite hatred and violence against women.[4] It's not just that women who like sex are 'bad', 'dirty' and 'naughty girls', feeding into all those messages we get about sex as not for respectable women. There is something much more hateful going on. Conducting in-depth linguistic analysis on online Incel forums, the study suggested that when Incels talked about sex – particularly between women and 'Chads', their name for masculine 'alpha' males – it was overwhelmingly in terms that echo those used in mainstream porn. Sex was described as something that was done to women, mostly by 'cocks' not people, and it was constructed in aggressive terms, with verbs such as 'choking', 'ravaging', 'beating', 'shoving' or 'pounding'. The study also found that both Incels and most of the porn it analysed used women's participation in sex as a way of insulting, degrading or dehumanizing them; often by reducing them to 'holes' or 'dumpsters' for men's ejaculation. And sex was regularly characterized by both Incels and mainstream porn as a form of punishment for women, a way of getting back at them for not doing or being as men desired. There's no way for us to know if there is a clear driver here; is it the Incels shaping the language in porn, or the porn shaping the Incels? But the connections between the two need more thought, especially because it isn't the only study to find problems with the way most porn talks about women. In 2016, research seeking to measure the scale of online misogyny analysed just under 1.5 million tweets sent over a period of twenty-three days containing the words 'slut' and 'whore'.[5] Over half of these tweets were advertising porn. Not only is this a startling figure considering that Twitter's minimum-age requirement is thirteen – making a mockery of the idea that children can't access porn online – but it goes to show that a lot of pornography could legitimately be considered a form of online misogyny. It's this detail that can be missing from the general sex positive position on porn, a position that, like Abigail, sees porn as a tool to challenge the shaming of sex. We've clearly still got work left to do before we lose the judgement surrounding women's sexual practice. But whether most porn helps or just embeds that judgement deeper is a question we need to keep asking.

Born to lesbian parents and a lesbian herself, Maddie felt that she was labelled a prude by people her age if she said anything vaguely critical of porn and the impact that she thought it was having. At nineteen she really needed the room to discuss what she was thinking, but whenever she tried to do it she felt that she was shut down. 'I think you can be critical of something that shapes sex but that doesn't mean you're being critical of sex,' she said. 'There's no space to discuss things freely without being scared of being brandished a bigot. From my individual experience in my university feminist society there's no way to have political discussions about sex and sexuality in a measured and mature way.' It was one of the reasons she wanted to talk to me in the first place; she said she needed to talk to someone about her experiences and not be branded 'anti-sex'. She was frustrated by a context which she felt wouldn't allow for anything other than a positive outlook and that closed off the complexities that come with all of our sexual experiences, including those that we have with porn. 'I think that pornography is often used as an educational tool to depict this is what sex is like, if you're not doing it this way then you're doing it wrong,' she said. 'So, if you're a woman sleeping with other women the only depiction you have of that in porn is two very feminine women fucking each other. It's so objectified, it's so sexualized, it's just so different from what it is actually like. But it overlaps into real life because if you are a lesbian there's so many men who think they can get involved in some way. I've had men wanting threesomes or jokes like, "Ooo, can I watch?" I think that pornography is fundamental to shaping those behaviours in real life.'

Blair came from a born-again Christian family who sent her to an Evangelical school with a fundamentalist position on sex. When it came to talking to the pupils about what happens in the bedroom, her school brought in an external provider whose messaging was so dangerous there'd been public cautions against using them. Blair was in her mid-twenties when we spoke but she remembered it as if it had happened yesterday. 'There was a particular group that came in to do the sex ed at school and the NHS had put warnings out about them because their information was so bad. They said things like, "condoms don't work, just abstinence" and put up pictures of serious cases of genital warts, so I spent most of the lessons breathing slowly, trying not to faint,' she said. 'The other thing they did was glued two pieces of paper together then ripped them apart so they were all mangled and torn. Then they said to us, holding up the shredded paper, "This is you if you have sex with someone, and then you break up."'

Instead of keeping them away from sex, all this shaming just meant that Blair and her friends felt bad about having it, summing up the reason a sex positive approach in schools is needed. But despite feeling critical of what she learned and how she learned it, she also thought the pendulum had swung towards a different kind of pressure. Like Maddie, she believed that sex positivity had become part of the problem. 'There's that extremism on one side,' she said, 'that if you think one impure thought, you might as well have gone around sleeping with everyone round the country. But there's also a pressure with the sex positive movement that women should be all right with everything. A lot of women think that they have to be the "cool girl" and act as if everything is permissible. Like that all men are interested in porn and women just have to put up with it. I just don't think that's true.'

Both Maddie and Blair in different ways were caught on the same tightrope: not only plagued by the vision of the respectable woman but also a new mythical creature who is sexually liberated and OK with anything as long as it's between consenting adults. To be her is to be always up for it and never say no. It's a different kind of pressure. But not to be her is to be frigid. And nobody wants to be that. The movement for sex positivity has tried to shift the negativity that surrounds women having and wanting sex. But it has also imposed a particular story of porn as empowering for women, and that has made it harder for us to point out when it isn't.

What we do with porn

Bonita was born into a loving Nigerian family in London. Like Jade, she told me that when she was growing up sex had always been pitched as something for men, but unlike Jade she grew up in the age of the internet. At fifteen she decided she needed to find out more and knew exactly where to go. 'I was very intrigued and I liked to explore,' she told me. 'So, I was just like, "Let me learn about sex." I went onto Google, free porn came up, and I just watched anything and everything.' Bonita used porn like a lot of straight women her age; not just to learn about what sex was but to find out what was expected of her by men. 'I remember I wanted to learn how to give head and I was on it a lot, trying to just watch the techniques,' she said. 'Or I'd hear men talking about how a woman needs to know how to ride, and I'd be like OK, that's the expectation of me. So, I'd go and look that up.' She told me that for the longest time she thought she was supposed to like having her hair pulled in sex; that anytime she watched porn that's what the man was doing, so she thought that was what she was meant to do. It was only when she was older that she felt she could say she didn't like it, and that's part of why – at sixteen – she said sex started to feel scary. 'A lot of the time we didn't even realize that a lot of the boys didn't know what they were doing,' she said. 'They were learning from porn and we were following them. Whatever he's doing or whatever he wants, that's what we do. We react after he acts. We just conformed and let be whatever be.'

I can remember feeling sad when she said this; to be honest I still feel the same. It's like Bonita – and the boys – had something taken from them, like they'd been cheated out of that starting-out phase where you're making it up together. Maybe it's because I'm getting older and look back on those days with rose-tinted glasses; I'm sure it wasn't as easy as I remember. But I never felt scared of sex – I didn't really know what it was till I had it. I first slept with a boyfriend when I was fourteen and neither of us had any idea what we were doing. We fumbled our way through it for months, in fact, finding what felt good and what definitely didn't. It wasn't the best sex I've had by a mile, but it felt like it was my sex to have. These days it sounds like it feels different, the porn seems to come first – accessed earlier and easier. I'm sure it could be making those first times better; it's probably less awkward if you've seen it all before. Still, I can't help but feel something's been taken from young people without them even knowing it. It's that messy making-it-up-together part, and there's no way to get it back.

To understand what was happening for Bonita and the boys, experts used to talk about cause and effect; the idea that watching porn causes people to want or to have sex in particular kinds of ways. These days, however, this view has fallen out of fashion, mostly because it oversimplifies the complex relationship that we have to the media we use. Instead, you're much more likely to hear people talking about something called 'sexual script theory'. Sexual scripts are the basic stories we tell ourselves about sex – what it is, what and who it's for, what acts are pleasurable, that kind of thing. They provide us with rules for determining in advance what's appropriate (or inappropriate) for us to do sexually, like how Jade thought sex was just supposed to happen in a loving relationship or how Bonita thought she was supposed to have her hair pulled. Scripts can differ between individuals based on a number of factors, but particular scripts are culturally dominant. These tell us the generally accepted story of sex and it's this that teenagers are often trying to work out.

Using this theory to think about porn and its relationship to what we do or think about sex often relies on what's been called the acquisition, activation, application model (3AM) of sexual socialization.[6] The idea is that porn can provide people who use it with scripts they're not aware of (the first A: acquisition); it can prime or reinforce scripts they are already aware of (the second A: activation); and it can encourage or discourage someone using particular scripts depending on how they're presented (the third A: application). Basically, watching porn provides us with particular stories about sex which can shape but don't determine our actions and attitudes. If we are watching something fairly regularly that is telling us a consistent story about what sex is and what is pleasurable in it, then it can start to feel like we need to match it. It can shape what we think of as 'normal'.

This way of understanding the relationship between the porn we watch and what we do can be useful in making sense of what's different for young people learning through porn today. Think back to Almina, who talked about seeing the number of views on a video and thinking this meant that that's what sex was and that's what kind of body was desirable. Access to porn these days is no longer limited to magazines, videos and DVDs, and the sheer volume of people using the sites creates the sense that what's being shown there represents most people's sexual lives. Some young people are picking up on this before they're actually having sex themselves. It's not hard to see how that plays out in this mass market version of sex, but as Bonita's story shows, it's hard to see it when you're in it. The girls are working out what's expected of them and the boys are working out what to expect of the girls and no one is seeing that these expectations are pretty different from the ways that sex can actually be. It was something that Sarah had encountered in her role as a sexual health advisor.

Sarah was in her fifties now and told me that she'd noticed a change over time from porn being somewhat on the outskirts, to becoming the dominant story for teenagers of what sex is. 'I'll give you an example,' she said. 'There was a young woman of school age and she was saying that she wasn't ready to lose her virginity, but her boyfriend had said that if they had sex anally that that would be OK, and she'd still be a virgin. And I was quite struck at the time by these young people saying that anal sex was not a big deal. And I'm not judgemental about it, you know — anyone can do what they want to do, if they both want to do it — but when I was young, all of this stuff was niche. Now it just seems like every bit of porn that I see goes into this formulaic thing of choking, throttling, spitting, slapping, you know;

this view that women are receptacles for men's pleasure and fluids. It upsets me that kids don't have the experience to understand that that isn't how it is supposed to be, and that there isn't even a "supposed to be". All they're seeing portrayed is this empty, mass market version.'

Concern about porn being used as a replacement for age-appropriate, accurate sex education is commonly dismissed as some kind of moral panic that says more about our regressive approach to sex than it does about pornography. And though the words 'moral panic' can be used much like 'hysteria' to dismiss the concerns of women, when it comes to porn and young people at least part of me can get behind the argument. There is some research supporting the idea that seeing porn as a teenager isn't always, or only, a bad thing. Despite the fact that officially pornography is only meant for adults, it's now fairly well accepted worldwide that children and young people use it, often to supplement a somewhat lacklustre sex education. A study on both rural and urban populations in Ethiopia and Uganda found that roughly 90 per cent of young people had seen porn before the age of eighteen, with 50 per cent of kids in Uganda seeing it before the age of twelve. When their reasons for doing so were explored in focus groups, the vast majority said they turned to pornography because they lacked adequate sex education. This was echoed in a nationally representative sample of Americans aged between eighteen and twenty-four which also found that, while they were growing up, pornography was seen as the most helpful source of information about how to have sex, even when compared to things such as sexual partners, friends, media and healthcare professionals. And it's the same in Britain, where an online survey commissioned in 2019 for the BBC asked more than 1,000 18–25-year-olds about their relationship with porn. Almost 80 per cent of young men and 50 per cent of young women said they'd watched porn in the last month, but more importantly 55 per cent of young men and close to 35 per cent of young women said porn had been their main source of sex education, something that was echoed recently in a 2023 report from the Children's Commissioner.[7]

It looks like, whether it should be or not, we can no longer claim that porn isn't a primary source for young people who want to learn about sex. And, though we might have a necessary tendency to focus on the harmful things young people could be learning, there's a small but growing body of research suggesting there might be some beneficial lessons there too. An Australian study in 2017 found that although around 87 per cent of the 800 young people surveyed had seen porn before the age of eighteen, the age of first exposure was much younger for not only boys – as we might expect – but also for young people who weren't heterosexual. This connects to other research findings that porn has helped young LGBT+ people (particularly, though not only, young gay men) understand and explore their sexuality, something that might be behind the fact that kids who aren't straight seem to access porn more than their heterosexual friends.[8] But it's not just for queer young people that researchers think porn might have some educational benefit. Researchers from the UK, Australia and America have argued that people of all sexualities can develop more egalitarian ideas about sexuality and gender by watching porn. They suggest that instead of the intense concern surrounding porn and young people, we should be thinking about it as a useful tool for them to develop a sense of sexual curiosity, imagination and adventure; a way to push back on conservative control over sex as something dirty and meant just for reproduction.

Dolores had seen some of this possible benefit when she worked as a teacher's assistant back in 2012. It meant she'd had a front-row ticket to how awful some sex education classes can be, which made porn as education seem like possibly the better option. 'I was in a sex ed lesson in secondary school and one of the kids put their hand up and asked a question,' she said. 'They asked, "So, the condoms, if you use two, would that be doubly effective? Like if you put one on top of the other?" And the teacher said, "Yeah. It probably would be, wouldn't it?" I'm so glad I was there because I had to be like, "No no no! That is not correct. Sorry, Miss, to contradict you there, but in fact that would make it much more likely to split. So, don't do that, definitely don't do that. You can get extra-thick ones, though." And these are people who are delivering sex education, not knowing the basics about condoms.' Dolores's experience wasn't all that long ago in the grand scheme of things, and given that the government in England has since rolled out mandatory relationships and sex education without training for those who are delivering it, I'm sure there are kids in school today being given the same kind of misinformation. But though they might not have someone like Dolores there to jump in with the facts when needed, they do all have access to porn. It makes sense that they're using it to supplement their education, and that's something that Dolores thought might actually be quite useful.

Fifteen years ago, Dolores was in the position of that kid, with lots of questions about sex that no one knew how to answer. She told me she first saw what felt like pornography on television late at night. It was actually something that came up for a number of women her age – Channel 4, Channel 5 and Eurotrash as replacements for what's now online. 'Mid-teens I remember seeing things on Channel 4 which were semi-pornography, slightly exploitative, late-night TV with softcore stuff which I was quite fascinated by, to be honest,' she said. 'Then when I was sixteen, I got into a sexual relationship with another girl and I'd never really properly masturbated before that but we sort of worked out how together. That was when I started having much more of a sex drive; I'd not really considered it up to that point. That was when I started masturbating and it was around that time that I started looking up porn.' She said that part of her reason for looking at porn was to understand a bit more about female anatomy, where everything was, or what it did, which porn helped her learn. That experience as a teenager, combined with what she had seen now in schools, meant she thought that porn might have a more useful role for young people than we usually give it credit for. 'There's a discussion people have: "Oh, kids are getting all their sex education from porn and that's terrible and something else should be happening,"' she said. 'And it's like, "Well, frankly, kids are going to get, from some porn, a much better sex education than they're going to get in school."'

Pornhub seems to agree. In 2020, it set up its own sex education site with five-minute videos explaining such things as female and male bodies, vaginal discharge and periods, STDs/STIs, and communication in sex. Though not directly advertised for under-eighteens, the videos focus on such basic information that it's hard to see how they aren't meant for people who haven't yet had sex. And that's where it gets a bit concerning. Because while the site comes from a firmly sex positive position – the videos extol the benefits of sex and definitely don't adopt the 'have sex once and you're broken' story that women like Blair learned at school – when you actually click on them, you're taken to a page which advertises the usual content on Pornhub. Which means that while there's no ripped paper or enlarged photos of genital warts to suffer through, there's more 'bad girls' and 'stepmoms' with 'facefuls' of cum than anyone needs to see when trying to learn how to put on a condom.

Martha felt that this, the actual content of the free porn that young people will first access, meant that the possible benefits of porn as an educational supplement were outweighed by its harm. She was almost forty when we spoke and told me that she used porn as an adult to help overcome the sex ed that she got in school. She felt porn helped her to think about sexual pleasure for women, something that as a Black woman she didn't think was encouraged. 'School was hilarious actually,' she told me. 'I remember one girl said, "Where's the clitoris, Miss?" My teacher turned beetroot. Sex wasn't about pleasure, it was about shame. Particularly for girls and particularly the Black community. We were shamed into behaving.' This point about shame being racialized is key, but can be lost sometimes in talking about women – as I often do here – as one big group. The myths, pressures and stereotypes that women face about sex can differ depending on our social positions. It means that though we're all in the same storm, we're weathering it in different boats. But while Martha agreed that porn could offer a counter-narrative to a conservative story of sex, she thought you needed to come to it with your own sexual experiences first, with some version of your own template that could help you distinguish the real from the fake. 'I've always thought pornography has a place, but where it's negative, where it's damaging, is for people who aren't able to understand the level of fantasy about it,' she said. 'Like the fact that they are young and are being influenced and they are still forming their own views and opinions. I would not want to be a sixteen- or seventeen-year-old girl now. I think in some ways it's got worse for girls with the access to pornography. I don't actually have a problem with pornography in general. What I do have a problem with is particular types of pornography that we have now and the fact that that may be the main source of sexual education for our young people growing up.'

Though she'd used it to affirm the fact that sex is for enjoyment, she thought that today most porn said something different, a story about sexual pleasure as coming from sexual violence. 'It's devoid of reality, completely, and it's violent. Not all of it, but a lot of the mainstream stuff that you can pick up in two clicks,' she said. 'You can see a woman being choked; you can see a woman being abused. Actually, quite horrific things which people think are normal. And it's being normalized at a time for young people when their sexuality is just coming up. You've got girls who are waxing everything and expecting to be in some porn star performance and they're not developing an enjoyment of sex or their bodies, just for themselves.' Porn might be helping young women be open to sexual possibility, but it looks like it's still not about their sexual pleasure.

Eleanor talked to me in detail about her experience of this, saying that all through her teens and into her twenties she watched porn, and a lot of it. 'I watched a lot of porn when I was younger. I watched porn solo, with friends, and then as I got older I watched porn with partners,' she said. 'My husband says I'm the only woman he's ever met that came into a relationship with her own porn collection. I brought my own videos because I didn't like his.' In her mid-thirties when we spoke, a white woman married with kids, her attitude to pornography had changed. She still watched it every now and then, but her reasons had shifted and it meant she was more critical of the story of sex it had told her. 'I know that when I watched porn as a teenager, I used to think it's incredibly liberating. I think part of it was show-ing I wasn't in the girl club, and part of it was for male attention,' she told me. 'For a long time when I had male partners it would be about per-formance. It would all be about putting on a show for them. I wouldn't think about whether I was enjoying it. It's so fucked up.' Though she didn't do that so much in sex any more, she still felt that porn was having an impact; that the scripts she'd acquired from porn as a kid were playing out in her desire. 'I think there's a real move towards the idea that if something feels good not to ques-tion why it feels good, that people aren't prepared to think about where their desires might come from and what they might actually be reflective of. It's the idea that power and a power imbalance is erotic. That's really difficult to unpick because it goes right to the core of how sexuality is shaped,' she said. 'I mean, I'm a woman now, but it's all still there when I have sex, those images seep into my mind. They're disturbing but I find them arousing. It's like porn has wound its way into my sexuality.'

What porn does to men

The statistics on how many men watch porn are pretty overwhelming. Studies looking at the percentage of men who have watched porn in the past year range from around 60 to 70 per cent in countries such as Italy, Australia, Egypt and Bangladesh, to something much closer to 90 per cent in the USA.[9] Here in Britain the most recent poll conducted by YouGov found that, of a nationally representative sample, 76 per cent of men say they've watched porn, with around a third watching it weekly, and 13 per cent watching it pretty much every day. Unsurprisingly, the rate at which men use porn decreases as you go up in the age brackets, though the YouGov poll found this wasn't as pronounced as you might expect, with around two thirds of men under thirty saying they watch porn and still one third watching porn over the age of sixty. Accumulating evidence is also suggesting that this watching is not having an altogether positive impact on their sex lives.[10] A review of the literature published in 2019 found that, overall, men who use porn regularly tend to report less satisfaction with their sex lives than those who use it rarely or not at all. There have been reports of porn contributing to sexual problems such as erectile dysfunction, delayed ejaculation, decreased sexual satisfaction and diminished libido, particularly in heterosexual men under forty, and repeated studies find a connection between men's porn use and poor mental health, including such things as significant levels of depression (though they can't be sure which one is the driver).

What's often missed in these studies looking at the sexual impacts for men is that, for men who have sex with women, they're not the only ones being affected. This was part of the reason why, for Arshi, porn was a dealbreaker in her relationships with men. It wasn't just about what they did with it alone, it's the way it infiltrated her sex life through them, and the barriers it put up in a relationship. Arshi was in her mid-thirities, an Indian woman with a British passport, 'one of the colonizers now', as she put it. She told me she held what people had said was a militant stance on porn, a sense that porn was a faultline between what she'd accept and what she wouldn't. It wasn't something that she felt confused by; she was resolute in her rejection. 'My value system deeply applies to me and my sexual life, and my attitude to porn is part of that,' she said. 'But people are more worried about where their eggs come

from than how women are treated and represented in porn. It's one of the most intimate
aspects of your being, and you're excluding your
values from it? It's bollocks. With men who use
porn I don't care if I like them, if this is what you
think of women then fuck off, I'm not interested.
Which perhaps is not a very inclusive position to
take but it has taken me a long time to come to
that, and I am proudly quite rigid about it.' Arshi
told me she felt porn was changing the sex men
wanted to have; that there were generations of
men who were being harmed, brought up on
equations of arousal with aggression. She said
that in her experience, porn made men struggle
with real intimacy. Though many women weren't
as resolved as she was, they'd definitely experienced something similar.

Clare was a dancer in her mid-thirties who
embraced what she called 'a nude lifestyle'. She
did almost everything naked from hiking to cook-
ing and was passionate about the need for us to be
more in tune with the body in its natural state.
Despite this, Clare came to watching porn herself
quite late by today's standards. She was raised as
a Catholic, and though she wasn't religious any
more, some of the messages she said she got about

sex from her faith were never far away. 'I probably started looking at pornography when I was
maybe thirty-one or thirty-two,' she said. 'Never,
ever looked at it before. I didn't have a smartphone for years and no laptop and no interest in
it, really. I was brought up as traditional Catholic
and a lot of the feelings of guilt and repression
still stay with me, to this day. So, it was a revelation
when I got an iPhone and I said, "What is all this
porn that everyone says is available on the internet?"' She couldn't remember who she was talking
to but someone told her she can just type it in. She
went home, typed in 'free porn' and basically was
blown away. 'I was horrified and amazed and
intrigued and I started watching it, I have to confess, which I wouldn't have thought I would have
done,' she said. 'It's interesting that I feel I have to
confess that to you. I don't have any shame in the
fact that I do it, but I still feel obligated to apolo-
gize.' For the next few years, Clare used porn off
and on, just the mainstream sites. Fast-forwarding
to the bits she wanted to see, trying to avoid the
violence – something she increasingly felt desensitized to. But it wasn't so much her own porn story
that she wanted me to know when we spoke, it
was more about her experience with a partner in a
relationship that was just ending.

'I've been with my partner for a couple of years and we're separating at the moment,' she said. 'He has erectile dysfunction; he's had it the whole time that we've been together and what turned him on was seeing me sleeping with other people. I was like, "Are you sure?" He was, "Yes. I really want you to do it." So, I went out and slept with other people and videoed it and took pictures and sent it to him and he thought that this was the best thing that he'd ever come across.' Clare told me she did it because he wanted her to; she felt pleasure from pleasing him. But she didn't really get anything from the encounters herself; it wasn't really something she wanted. He then said that it wasn't fair that she'd been sleeping with other people and he wanted to do it too, so they signed up to a swingers site, which he started spending a lot of time on. 'When we first moved, we didn't have any internet and a few weeks later I came across a conversation that he'd been having privately with a girl on the site,' she told me. 'He'd said to her, "I can't believe that we've got no internet and I've got nothing to masturbate to and it's really shit." I thought, "I'm your girl-friend and we've just moved into our dream place in the countryside and is this why we haven't had sex for the last week? Because you've had no porn?"' She confronted him about it and they had a massive fight and then things started getting worse. On the swingers site people were more interested in her than him, he got more depressed, and their sex life dwindled to nothing. 'Then the other day I said to him, "You really ought to get counselling." And he said, "I had counselling for eighteen months when I was addicted to pornography and it didn't help." So, turns out he was addicted to porn.'

It hurt Clare to hear this because he'd never told her that before. But it also made sense of a lot of what had been happening in their sex life; porn had never been far away and she thought it probably had had an impact that even he wasn't fully aware of. 'I think the fact that he was addicted had a massive influence not just on his erectile dysfunction but also on the fact that he wanted me to go off doing all these crazy things,' she said. 'A lot of the time, I'd be giving him a blowjob and he'd have to get the iPad out to finish himself off. If you have to watch a video of a threesome to come, not as a one-off but on a regular basis, then that, to me, says something's changed in the wiring of your brain. He organized a gang bang for me once. I was like, "How romantic." But I idolized him and I still do. I just wanted to do anything to keep him happy.'

I was in touch with Clare recently and she told me that not long after we spoke, she'd started coming to terms with the fact that her ex had been abusive. Looking back on the relationship, she thought it was incredibly unhealthy and that what she'd seen in porn played a part in that; it made his controlling behaviour harder to recognize. 'I accepted it so readily at the time,' she said, 'yet I can now see how screwed up it was. I think that porn and the pressurized situations it depicts is so normalized that it makes you feel that it is common practice, even if you've never experienced that sort of sex yourself before. But that's coercive control – you're a very gradually boiled frog, hoping that the water must start cooling down soon, so you just hang on that little bit longer.'

Clare's experience was at the sharp end of something a lot of women who had sex with men said. That porn was coming into the bedroom through the practices of their partner. It wasn't only about addiction, gang bangs and swingers. It filtered in through the everyday ways that some men wanted to have sex. Amelia, who had found the boxes of porn under her boyfriend's bed, spoke about how porn influenced the sexual practices of the partners that came after. 'I can definitely tell when we're having porn sex, so to speak; I can see when a man switches off from the connection and starts pretending like he's in a movie,' she said. 'When my current partner and I first got together, every now and again he would slap my bottom, try and put his finger in it and spit on my vagina. And also, something I've had with many previous sexual encounters is the whole grabbing of the hair or the grabbing of the head, and just ramming your head into their penis when you're trying to give them a blowjob.' She said that she hated that in particular as it made her feel really restricted, like she didn't have control over her own movement, but it was something from her experience that was exceptionally common. 'I had a word with my partner actually when he kept slapping my bum. I would say I didn't want him to do that and then he would do it again. So, I spoke to him about it and he was like, "Oh, you never said that you didn't want me to do that," and I was like, "I'm sure this is the third time I've said this,"' she told me. 'But I think that for some reason women have this real desire to please, and even if they are being hurt, they don't want to say anything because they don't want to ruin the moment.'

Stine also had a fair bit of experience when it came to how men brought porn into the bedroom. It was something that she watched herself regularly so she'd become good at spotting it. 'I've said it to one of my recent ones; I just turned around after sex and I went, "You watch a lot of porn, don't you?"' she said. 'And he was like, "Yes, I actually do," and I was like, "Yes, I can tell."' In her mid-twenties now, Stine had overcome her strict white Pentecostal upbringing, and had got to a place where she felt comfortable with sex and knew what she liked and why. She told me there were certain things that gave her an indication that a man had watched too much porn – narrating what they were doing was one, as was wanting to come on her face, which came up for a lot of women, and anal sex, which was something she said she did, but not when men just spat on her butt hole and expected to gain entry. 'Porn has really cracked away at the anal stuff, and now if you don't do it, it's like a cross against your name,' she said. 'I've been seeing a guy and he tried the other day. I stopped him mid-sex and I said, "If you ever, ever try and put something in my bum hole without prior permis-

sion and lube, I will be leaving with your balls." '
She told me she'd had to get more assertive
because otherwise she just wasn't going to get
what she wanted. She'd had to unlearn that desire
to please and was now happy to ruin the moment
if she had to. 'I've walked out before,' she told
me. 'I've walked out during sexual encounters
when I've tried to give pointers and they've
ignored it. I've said, "I'm not enjoying that,"
politely, and then more like, "No, that actually
hurts." Then they keep on and it's like, "OK. Just
get the fuck off me, I'm going home." '

It was the recognition that porn was seeping into
the sex she was having, whether she wanted it to
or not, that led Cindy Gallop, the founder of
MakeLoveNotPorn, to create a porn site where
members can access and submit videos of sex that
are free of porn clichés. In a much-discussed
TED Talk from 2009, Gallop explored how porn
had become a default form of sex education for
men and how she'd seen this first hand in the sex
that she had as a woman in her fifties with men
three decades younger.[11] It was something that
Imogen spoke about with real insight, how
having sex with younger men really showed the
ways that porn was changing sexual practices.

Imogen was a white woman in her early forties who worked for many years in the sex industry. She told me she stopped about five years ago because her partner didn't want her to do it any more, but she brought her understanding of the industry to the porn she watched and the experience of the women in it. It meant she didn't have the conflict others did about what they were watching, and when I asked why that was, she said that basically, sometimes, there's no downside. 'All I can say to other women is don't always assume that there's exploitation,' she said. 'Yes, you should be aware that it can happen, but if it looks like she's enjoying herself and she's in control of what's going on, then accept it for what it is. She probably loves what she does and she's got a very good lifestyle. It might just be what she wanted to do since she was seventeen, eighteen, because it's what I wanted to do when I was that age. I made my choice to do it, no one coerced me. I loved what I did and I miss it every day.' When Imogen was working, she didn't watch porn herself, though now she said it was very much part of her daily life. Back then she felt she had no personal need for porn because she'd be watching it with clients and got to do the things that she'd be fantasizing about so she didn't think that there was much point. But even though while she was working she wasn't watching porn herself, she'd noticed a clear difference in the sexual practices of young men compared with their older counterparts. She attributed most of it to porn. 'Despite my age, I did used to have quite a lot of young clients, eighteen, nineteen. And my perception and experience is that young men have a warped view of what sexual relationships are because of the kind of stuff that they have watched,' she said. 'There is this sense that women are the inferior person in the relationship and that they are there only to give pleasure. If that means that he throws her around the bed and puts her in eight different positions and comes on her face or whatever, that's fine, because that's what women are for. That's my concern; because those things are portrayed as being "normal", as being just what women do. I'm concerned that there is an expectation from young men for all women to behave like that.' Annemarie had seen the same thing.

Annemarie was white like Imogen and only slightly older. She'd used the internet to enter the sex industry, making amateur porn first by herself and then later with her boyfriend. She talked about how far she'd come to feel comfortable doing that, and the shaming messages she got when she was young about sexual pleasure and her body. 'As a child I was forever being told off for having my hand down my pants and quite publicly shamed for masturbating, which my mum referred to as "picking at your bottom",' she told me. 'My mum would smell my hands to see if I'd been masturbating. It's so fucking dysfunctional when I look back.' She didn't understand for years that sex was something people had for pleasure, or the reasons it felt good when she put her hands down her pants. She told me finding that out was a watershed moment. She never really looked back.

Fast-forward forty years and Annemarie was somewhere very different. She'd started making porn of herself, putting it online to make some extra cash, and everything just grew from there. 'I guess my first forays into making porn were on my own. I just thought maybe I should record some of my sessions and put them up to see if it could be a little money-spinner,' she said. 'I just recorded a couple of short videos of me masturbating, without showing my face, and they sold really well. So, I thought, "Wow, this is great, I'll make some more."' A little while later, Annemarie met her boyfriend, who was an amateur photographer at the time, so he did a few shoots for her. And then she figured eventually people would get bored of the masturbation, so she suggested they could branch out and do something with the two of them in together. He was up for it. 'I think the first one we did was after we got to talking about if we were going to do a porn video, what would we do. I think up until then we'd done a couple of clips that had just been like three minutes of us fucking and then a cum shot, and I wanted something longer that would be more profitable.' They ended up filming something of a classic porn scenario where her boyfriend played a customer who'd arrived at a high-end restaurant and found the staff were having sex when they should have been taking his order. So, he'd called the manager – played by Annemarie – to complain and she ended up saying, 'Sir, what can I do to stop you leaving a bad review?' 'It was so cheesy,' she said, 'but it was actually really hot filming it and I think part of the hotness was that it was so fucking clichéd. Normally I'm quite dominant, I don't put up with any bullshit from sex partners, whether they are clients or private partners. But this gave me permission to explore a different facet of my sexuality and feel more comfortable about doing that.'

While she didn't say explicitly that she'd sold sex – and I didn't notice it at the time to clarify – Annemarie talked about having clients as sexual partners, and when mentioning the younger ones in particular, what she had to say echoed Imogen. 'I've noted it that when I've had clients under the age of about twenty-five, they seem to expect this kind of porn star performance,' Annemarie told me. 'It's like they think that they're going to deep-throat you and that they can take hold of your head and just fuck your face without asking, or spit on your vulva as lubrication. I've sat there before and gone, "Did you just spit on my vagina, young man? That is not OK," and they're kind of like, "Oh, isn't it?" They really don't know. I've had to say, "Of course it's not OK, you don't spit on somebody without permission, for Christ's sake, I've got a bottle of lube right here." And they just go, "Oh, I didn't realize." I think there is definitely a tendency for that kind of thing in sex with younger guys.'

Both Imogen and Annemarie thought that what the younger men were doing was symptomatic of what most porn says about women. It was that same old idea again, that we're only there to respond to men, not to participate ourselves. Imogen said that she wasn't sure they'd act the same with a woman they hadn't booked, but she felt like the way they treated her wasn't about them paying, it was about their expectations of women in general. 'I think that was really where my concern kicked up a notch,' she told me. 'I thought, "Oh my God, we're just turning all these young men into sexual fiends." To the point that I would even qualify at the end of a booking and say, "Well, that was great fun, but you do realize that you wouldn't treat your girlfriend that way." Which they used to laugh at because then they'd sort of say, "Oh, you can't say that." And I'd say, "I can, darling. I'm old enough to be your mother."'

There's a lot of campaigning that goes on with young people saying porn isn't the same as sex. It's about separating reality from fantasy and putting porn firmly in the box of the latter. But when you listen to women's experiences, the two regularly overlap. It provides us with a road map but can also be a form of escape. It has a role in expectation or imagination or both. We take what it teaches us into our lives, it helps us explore and sometimes holds us back. We need to be able to tell both sides of the story if we're going to make sense of it all. In a society where nobody talks about sex, porn has become the authority on what we do and how we do it, on what's pleasurable and why. It's not the only message we get but we're also not the only ones taking it in. It means that porn plays a part in shaping us sexually, whether we like it or not.

RELATIONSHIPS

Using porn with partners

IN THE PENULTIMATE SEASON OF *Friends*, one episode – 'The One With the Sharks' – details the reaction of a popular character to her partner watching porn. The notoriously uptight Monica Geller, played by Courtney Cox, surprises her husband, Chandler, who is away overnight for work. Monica sorts out an extra key and enters his hotel room just as he has started watching pay-per-view porn. Seeing it now it's a little bit cringey but in that easy to watch, nostalgic way. The laughs are sometimes forced, the reactions often bizarre, but the plot carries us along without any effort. She enters, he jumps, and quickly changes the channel. She doesn't see the porn but does see he was getting ready to masturbate. She looks at the TV, which is now on a show about sharks, and the rest of the episode is her coming to terms with that being his secret kink. It all comes to a head a minute before the credits roll when Chandler returns home and Monica greets him, VHS in hand. 'This,' she says, 'is how much I love you,' before putting it in the tape deck, sitting down beside him and pressing play. He thinks it's porn. It's not, it's sharks. Hilarious confusion ensues. Then, mix-up resolved, he looks at her lovingly and says, 'You're amazing. You were actually going to do this for me?'

Whether we like it, hate it, or something in between, the idea that women watch porn only for men can feel like a bit of a cliché. It may be that the tide is turning; it's easier than ever for women to access porn themselves. But when I look back at the stories I've heard, I have to say men almost always form part of how we start. Rebecca, who was in her mid-forties when I met her, talked about what men's use of porn meant for women. She thought men's use made it almost impossible to avoid. 'Men bring it,' she said. And for the women I've talked to, it seems like she's right. Like Jade finding her dad's magazines, Makeda and her cousins, Almina and Lily and boys at school, Rowan and her dad. It was actually such a common thread in the stories women told me that I almost began to expect it. No matter whether they shared it on purpose or whether or not the women took it up themselves, the first time most women remembered seeing porn was because of the practices of men.

Aurelia was introduced to porn by a male partner and, much like me and *Nurse Nookie*, though it wasn't anything to write home about it wasn't an awful experience either. 'The first memory of porn that I have was with a boyfriend and I would have been about nineteen,' she told me. 'He introduced me to RedTube and we watched *The Art of Sex*. It was very much shown in the way of it being something he thought would be more appealing to me, something softer and not very hardcore. It wasn't amazing, but it wasn't bad either. I must have enjoyed it because I definitely went back.' Now twenty-five and some sexual partners later, Aurelia had continued using porn in relationships every now and then. And while she said it felt good using it with a partner, it was different when she was alone. 'I felt quite comfortable when I was doing it with my partner in a sexual way. I then explored it myself but had much more of a reaction,' she said. 'I couldn't look at the screen straight away. I felt way less comfortable. It felt wrong when I was by myself.' Alone, Aurelia had that sense of conflict, but it went away when she used porn with men.

The silence around what women do with porn is broken when it comes to watching it within our relationships. Here experts are almost crawling over each other to tell us what to do, and how, and why. We are told that watching porn together can be part of a healthy, happy sex life, that we can use it to get to know our partner better, that it can help reignite a waning spark. And it looks like some of this might be backed up by evidence. Though what using porn with a partner does for a relationship is still an open question, it does seem that in a mixed bag of research there's a consistent finding that there can be some benefits. Overall, studies seem to find that if romantic couples share pornography together, they report higher levels of sexual and relationship satisfaction than if just one partner is using it alone. But the issue with research is that there can be multiple explanations of the same data, and whether that satisfaction is about sharing porn or just not having the secrecy that so often goes along with one partner using it is yet to be determined.[1] It also might be a bit of a red herring. Because much like using feminist porn, watching porn with a partner – whether paid for or not – actually doesn't seem to be that common. The *Marie Claire* survey from 2015 on women's use of porn found that only 3 per cent of respondents watched porn with a partner regularly and two thirds had never even attempted to do so.[2] Academic studies say something similar, with a study from 2016 with over 1,500 heterosexual couples finding that the vast majority of women do not use porn often with their male partners, and over half haven't tried it with them at all.[3] It was much the same in the conversations I've had with women; male partners seemed to introduce it into the relationship, but not many women kept it up. At least not in the relationship itself.

Bonita, who had gone to porn first to learn how to ride, had also watched porn with a boyfriend, not regularly but a couple of times. And though she said it wasn't something she'd probably do again, at the time she found it quite useful. She told me that watching porn together was the first time she'd ever actually really sat down with someone and had a conversation about what they liked sexually. 'Before that it was just like a guessing game,' she said. 'And as we'd go along, we got used to each other's bodies. But we watched it together and said, "What do you like? What do you not like?" It was nice to have that conversation.' Ali had also done the same with several past partners, though she didn't do it with the man she was with now. She was a white woman in her early thirties, and one of the few women I talked to who spoke really positively about watching porn with a partner. For Ali it was about being comfortable, with yourself, your relationship, and with the porn you were watching. If you had that then she thought it could have real benefits, and beside that, she said, it was a fun thing to do. 'If you're going to watch porn together then it has to be something that you're both comfortable with. You need to talk first about what you like to watch and then find something you both like,' she told me. 'Sometimes you watch some things and it can be, "Oh, I'd like to try that." Or, "I really don't like that." Or, "I like that, I forgot to say." But I've always been quite horny, I've got quite a high sex drive, and it's kind of hot to watch it together, so why not?'

Although what's behind the high rates of sexual and relationship wellbeing for couples who use porn together isn't entirely clear, what comes up regularly is this sense of it helping sexual conversations. The idea here is that using porn together provides opportunities to learn about each other's sexual likes and dislikes; that seeing it on screen helps us to say it, and it's the speaking about it together that really helps drive that sense of satisfaction. But without that reciprocity it's just a one-sided conversation, and when that happens, women lose out. As Elizabeth discovered fairly quickly when she started sleeping with men.

Like Catherine, who came out as bisexual in her late twenties, Elizabeth had thought she was a lesbian for most of her life. Though she'd come far from that sixteen-year-old girl who thought she'd done something wrong when she first made herself orgasm, she said she still came to sex relatively late and first slept with a woman when she was twenty-eight. Four years later she found out that she wanted to have sex with men. It was something that porn had helped her explore, a way of coming to terms with her sexuality. 'I thought I was gay for a long time, and so that was all that I focused on, and then, when I became aware that I was hiding the fact that I was attracted to men as well, I started to talk to my friends about what guys like,' she said. 'But because I was a bit older, I was seen as a late bloomer. So rather than talking to people about it – because I found it very uncomfortable – I would just look at what I would see in pornography, and come to terms with my sexuality in a safe space by myself.' Once she felt ready, Elizabeth started sleeping with men. One of her first times, though, was a disaster and it shows how watching porn together can sometimes keep sexual partners apart. 'I was seeing this guy and he came over and wanted to watch porn before we had sex. I'd never done that with anybody else but I wasn't very experienced with men, so I thought that was the done thing,' she said. 'And literally, the reason he was interested in me was because he was aware that I was into women and he thought that I may just be interested in fucking anything that moves. I remember this whole build-up, we had a lot of text messages where we had been seductive and quite sexy, and I remember just being there with him watching it, and thinking, "I don't want to do what they're doing in that film with you. I want to be with you, I want to explore you, what you like and what I like. I don't want the film to turn you on, I want to be the one who does that."'

They didn't meet up again. Watching porn hadn't felt like something they were doing together; it had made Elizabeth feel like she was an extra part, that there didn't need to be an attraction or connection. She said she felt she'd done herself a disservice, that it gave her the sense that she didn't have to try; she could sit this one out and porn would do the work for her. 'Pornography can dumb down the messiness of sex,' she said. 'Sex isn't perfect, it's not like it's all great and we all climax together. And I think what porn put in my head was that I can't measure up to what's happening on the film, but if he watches that, he'll be pleased, so I don't have to perform.'

Jessica felt something similar. Though she didn't watch porn with her partner, she found something of a use for it within their relationship. When we spoke, Jessica was in her forties and said her sexuality had been buried after the birth of her first child two years ago. She said that sex was never discussed in any context in preparation for parenthood, but having a child was having a huge impact on her and the relationship she had with her partner. 'The birth of my child has drastically changed my sexuality and how in touch I am with it,' she said. 'It really does turn your world upside down, particularly if you're breast-feeding and you're taking prime responsibility for caring for the child, which is exhausting. It changes your whole identity but there's nothing to prepare you or your partner for that. Rather than seeing yourself sexually as a woman, you're more in touch with a new identity of being a mother and a carer. For me, that's led to a lot of tension.'

Jessica had mostly stayed away from porn as a kid, though her parents had *The Joy of Sex*, a book that graced the shelves of many homes in the eighties. At nineteen she moved in with her first boyfriend, who was in his mid-twenties, found his stash of magazines and threw them all in the bin. 'I suppose I had this naive take on relationships, at the time, that sex and sexual attraction is the key part of your relationship,' she said. 'And I felt probably a little bit, I don't know whether "jealousy" is the right word, but a little bit threatened, a little bit shocked that, actually, he was looking to other sources of pleasure or arousal that weren't with me.' Porn didn't really play much of a part again in that relationship or any others. Through her twenties she said her confidence grew and she became more comfortable with her body. Like many women, she felt she hit her sexual stride in her thirties, right when, as luck would have it, having a baby took most of her sexual desire. 'When I had my child, that was a period where I felt under a lot of pressure to have sex, when I wasn't emotionally, or physically ready. I was exhausted and felt unsupported,' she said. 'My partner moved into my house and, sometimes in the night when I got up for the toilet or to feed my child, I just got the impression that he'd been looking at porn. I felt almost like I wanted to creep downstairs, the TV would go quiet, you know, it was like, what's going on?' She told me they talked about it a few times but now her feelings on porn were more conflicted. She wasn't sure how it fitted into her relationship but she saw it had a purpose; to take a weight off her. 'Though my feelings were still on the negative side about porn in general, it was more like negative positivity,' she said. 'At one point I thought, "Actually, maybe it's fine." It was providing whatever he needed then and it took the pressure off me.'

Jane also knew the havoc that children can wreak on your sex life, but she'd taken a different approach to what that might mean for porn and her relationship. Jane had just turned thirty and was a researcher on sexual health and so she'd had more discussions than most about sex, masturbation and pleasure. She remembered being eight and watching *Body of Evidence*, a 1993 film featuring Madonna and an awful lot of sex scenes with her co-star Willem Dafoe. It wasn't exactly porn, but it felt like it at the time until at twelve or thirteen she found a box at the back of her dad's filing cabinet. 'My dad had this box of porn videos,' she said. 'He often worked late and he would leave me alone at home from the age of, like, twelve or thirteen. And whenever he went out, I would go and use those videos. I just liked the feeling they gave me.' She did that for quite a while, she told me, and then at seventeen started having sex herself. After that she took a break from porn, until years later – with her partner – she found what was online. She started using it again when she felt like it – which hadn't been all that much lately.

When we spoke, Jane was heavily pregnant with her second child; she went into labour just six days later. This time around, though, pregnancy had been much harder. It wasn't only about the baby coming, it was balancing that with the needs of her toddler, her career and her marriage. And, like Jessica, it meant that in the last few months she'd lost touch with her sexual desire. 'I'm due a baby next week, so I'm really not in the mood. I haven't been for a while,' she told me. 'Plus, this is my second baby so we have an idea that afterwards it's tough to get back in the saddle. So I was speaking to my partner last night about maybe getting a subscription to something like Erika Lust,' she told me. 'I registered on her website and you get a free clip and it was really sexy and sensual and nice. You could tell the woman was enjoying it and they were kind of good-looking but normal-looking people. So, I said to him, "Maybe when we're ready to get back on the game, we can buy one of her films." We're really stingy and I'd rather not pay. But I think that porn can help us get back into it.'

Using porn with a sexual partner can be a mixed bag. For some of us it's useful, for others it breaks the connection. But while most of the women I spoke to didn't use porn with other people, it was still a part of their relationships in one way or another.

Using porn for ourselves

A few years ago a large-scale research project conducted in England on how people use porn found a number of key gender differences in the data, such as men felt like porn was more important to them than women did, as well as using it more often and using more specialist sites. But it also found a key difference in terms of what porn did to desire. While men were more likely to use porn when they were already aroused, women tended to use it as a means to arousal.[4] And it's not the only study to have found this. Across the board it seems that although women view porn less frequently than men overall, they're more likely to feel an increased desire to have sex with their partner on a day that they use porn, and they're more likely to follow through with that desire. This finding that porn puts women in the mood for sex held for those in both mixed-sex and same-sex relationships. In other words, women in relationships seem to use porn as a sort of foreplay.

As a teenager, Alice just watched porn to see what everyone was talking about but she said she was never really that interested. Even now she told me she only watches woman-on-woman porn, that heteronormative porn is too violent, it gets complicated too quickly and she can't lose herself in it. When we spoke she was in her late twenties and had found a new purpose for porn. Over the last few years she'd discovered porn helped her to remember that she liked to have sex. She said she used it like a kick-starter, an accelerator into exploring her sexuality. It hadn't always been that way. 'When I was a young woman,' she told me, 'I thought porn was what sex looked like. All the negative tropes that porn puts out about how women have sex and what women enjoy. I thought women were supposed to have orgasms every time they saw a penis. It took me years to stop doing what I thought I was supposed to do during sex.'

Through her twenties Alice started having more conversations about sex and sexual desire, and it had changed how she felt about porn. That in turn had changed what it meant for her relationships, and now she used it to help them. 'I always used to think porn was a threat. I used to think that if my boyfriend was watching porn, and this is quite hard to say out loud because it makes me sad for myself, but I used to think if a boyfriend was watching porn, then I was not good enough or we weren't having sex enough,' she told me. 'But then the last five years I started to have more conversations and I began to own a lot more aspects of my sexuality. My boyfriend and I started to talk more openly about what we liked, didn't like and what we wanted, et cetera, and porn just came in when the doors were open.' It wasn't that her boyfriend initiated it, as for a good few years Alice had been watching porn herself. But she found it had a new purpose, and that was to help remind her that she wanted to have sex. 'Sometimes now we watch porn together, usually as a form of foreplay. I find it really helpful as a tool to get turned on,' she said. 'I don't have a very high sex drive, so often I am not that bothered. I am just not one of those people who walk down the street and goes, "I feel like having sex." So, it can be helpful as a way to connect with my sexuality because often when we start watching porn together I will physically respond. My body goes, "I remember. I really do like having sex."' Porn wasn't so much about getting off as it was about getting her started.

Myra had also used porn like this in the past, to help her get the party started. When we spoke, she'd just hit her forties and was married with two children still in primary school. The demands of parenthood meant that, along with a lot of personal pleasures, sex had become something they just had to grab when they could. Like Alice, Myra had been on a journey with porn, but this time the journey had moved her further away from wanting it in her life. It had meant that using porn for arousal didn't happen much these days, so she had to find a different way to get there on her own. 'When I was younger,' she told me, 'I watched porn a bit. I watched porn with boyfriends and watched porn with my husband and I did actually up until we had kids, but then it started to seem a lot seedier. I found internet porn, places like Pornhub, where people can upload any stuff that they want. And that's just made me think of it in a whole different light. I couldn't really find it a turn on unless the women were enjoying it, and finding women who enjoy it in porn these days is quite few and far between.'

Like Jessica, who found porn took the pressure off her after childbirth, Myra also felt she reached her sexual peak in her thirties. But this time luck was more on her side because during her second pregnancy her hormones went wild. 'I was just really turned on all the time,' she said. 'So, every day I would masturbate and watch porn. Totally hormonal.' She said that since having kids she started using porn to start herself off, to help get in the mood. 'With children now, obviously having sex during the day is a bit of a luxury,' she said. 'But if my husband was at work and I knew he was coming home, I'd put on some porn and masturbate a little bit before he got back. I think my orgasms would be quite heightened because I'd been warming up to it. That's the way I used it really, as a warm-up for sex.' Lately, though, it had become more difficult after she'd found a video on Pornhub of a woman being raped. She said it was a rude awakening and she hadn't gone back since. 'There were two guys, and you couldn't see their heads,' she told me. 'It was just their bodies and her, doped up. She's been raped on video and it's on the internet. I reported it when I saw it, but you just think, how many of those are there?' It meant she couldn't watch porn without being scared of what she'd see, and though she'd tried looking for more women-centred content, she didn't find anything she liked enough to have as part of her digital foot-print. 'So, I don't watch it myself now and the times that we've watched it together, it hasn't been very successful,' she said. 'I'm a bit like, "No, can't watch that now, can't watch that." It's not that my husband watches ultraviolent porn but he likes women giving head and taking, and I'm just a bit repulsed by it now.'

While both Alice's and Myra's partners were aware they were using porn in their relationships to help with arousal – mostly because they were also using it with them – that isn't always the case. Research has found that it is not unusual for one or both partners in a committed romantic relationship, irrespective of sex, to have a sexual secret, especially if it is considered beneficial to their maintaining boundaries and privacy. In 2021, a study that looked into this in more detail found that for its mostly female sample, along with past sexual experiences and our sexual fantasies, our own porn use was one of the topics women talked about the least with our intimate partners.[5] Sadie thought it all harked back to the suppression of women's sexuality.

Sadie was a dual-heritage woman who was nearly thirty, and had first seen porn with a partner back in her mid-teens. 'The first boyfriend that I had managed to get a DVD off his stepdad,' she told me. 'I think he found it under the bed or something; it was cheesy eighties porn. We watched it together, and I remember thinking, "I should be aroused by this", but I just found it uncomfortable, the whole situation was a little bit awkward.' As technology developed, Sadie started using porn on her phone. Usually, it was websites she'd been sent by another boyfriend but, even though she wasn't finding the porn by herself, at least this time it did what it was supposed to do. When Sadie used porn alone to masturbate, she was able to orgasm quite easily – though she did think, like Clare had said, she'd become desensitized to it over time. The porn had started to make it harder for her to fantasize without it, so like Leonora going back to the written word, Sadie had been trying recently to use more of her imagination. But when Sadie was having sex with men, she found it hard to finish. It was something that she thought made some men feel threatened; that she could give herself the pleasure they couldn't. 'For me personally, I can't climax through sex. I can only really do it by myself, and I've found that men find that difficult to accept,' she said. 'Every guy will have this thing, "Oh, don't worry, I'll change that" or "You've never met someone like me before." And I feel like I have to go through that motion of, "Oh, I'm close," when I'm not. I just know it's not going to happen.' It meant that sometimes during sex she'd fake it so her partner would feel good, then go home and use porn to quietly get herself off. 'I think there's something intimidating about a woman that can satisfy herself and doesn't need a male partner,' she said. 'It's that general suppression of women's sexuality. It can end up being about their ego more than about your pleasure.'

This suppression might also be behind a current research gap on the use of pornography alone by women who are in committed relationships.

There's been research suggesting that, as with the experiences of Myra and Alice, women in relationships who use pornography do so primarily to enhance their sexual relationships rather than to engage in a sexual experience of their own.[6] And this is what studies on women and pornography have historically focused on – where women's use has been asked about, it's often in the context of using it with a male partner. This is quite different to studies with men, which are much more likely to explore the fact that men in relationships do use porn for and by themselves. Despite the argument that some researchers have made that pornography should be understood as a relationship phenomenon, it still seems that when we're looking at heterosexual relationships, women's use outside of men's isn't considered that important. It means that not only do we not know how common it is for women in relationships to be using porn themselves, we also don't know that much about what this use might mean for them and their partner, or actually if their partner knows about it at all.

Siobhan was hiding her porn use from her long-term boyfriend. She was a white woman in her early forties, over a decade older than Sadie, but similar to the reasons behind Sadie lying about coming during sex, Siobhan hid what she was watching to protect her partner's feelings. For years, Siobhan had had depression and it had really affected her sex drive, while her partner also had some mental health issues, meaning their sex life had faded away to almost nothing. 'We haven't had sex together for a long time,' she said. 'We're intimate but we don't have penetrative sex, which I know isn't all of sex but I suppose it's what you measure it by.' Her partner regularly went away for work and sometimes when he was gone, and Siobhan got the urge, she'd watch porn. She liked a particular site set up by a woman called Lucie Blush in response to the focus on men and their pleasure that's found in most mainstream porn. Siobhan bought a subscription and then downloaded all the videos and cancelled her direct debit. Now she had a collection of films that she liked and that was all she used. But she wasn't using it in her relationship as a warm-up to sex so much as a replacement, and it's this that she couldn't tell her partner. 'What interests me is that my partner doesn't know about the films. I wouldn't mind if he found out or anything, but I don't think I would tell him,' she said. 'I think it boils down to our own mental health problems and not having sex for a long time. I think he would feel bad that I was able to get off on my own when he's not in the house because I'm not able or don't do those things with him now. But you know we've all got an errant in life that your intimate partner doesn't need to know. Even if you've been together a long time, there's stuff that you don't need to tell everybody.' Carol felt the same; even though when we talked she wasn't looking at much porn, it was still something she hid.

At almost forty, Carol said she'd had an off-and-on relationship with porn in the past, using it mostly when she wasn't with someone as a sexual outlet. But she always felt that conflict about it, between what she was watching and the ethics of it all. She didn't want to pay as she didn't use it enough, and it meant that what she was left with didn't always sit well with her. 'I can remember watching a documentary about a woman in porn and at the end of what she was doing she was in tears. That's just her working life, you know, but nobody cares, absolutely nobody working round her cares,' she said. 'All these guys had been doing whatever they were doing to her, and then after the act, it was back to the caravan. And the fact that nobody did anything on that documentary suggested to me that that is quite normal. I just found that really disturbing.'

In part because of this conflict and the sense of shame she felt about it, Carol had developed particular strategies for her porn use, all designed for secrecy. She had a private browser, deleted all her history, said she made sure that porn was 'dead and buried' on her laptop, even though at the time she was living alone. 'On my own laptop, in my own flat, there was still a kind of secrecy, I was hiding it,' she told me. This sense of needing to hide it continued even when Carol stopped using porn with any kind of frequency. She'd still have a look every now and then; she'd found a few sites that she thought represented women well and – though she'd have to pay to access them fully – she found what they gave you for free did the job. But even though she hardly used it any more and stayed off the mainstream sites, it still wasn't something she wanted to talk about with her partner, particularly now she was in a relationship with a woman. 'I think that having sex with a man, there tends to be a lot more focus on what he wants,' she said. 'Less so with another woman, it's far less judgemental. But there is still a sense of shame in admitting to my partner that

I've looked at porn because of the way that she says she feels about it. I wouldn't tell her and I wouldn't want her to know about it. I don't think she'd be comfortable with it.' Carol's reasons for keeping it hidden now were a bit like Siobhan's. It was an attempt to protect her partner from something she thought would make her upset. 'My feelings about it have got stronger, I think, because I'm in a happy relationship, and our sex life is a positive one. But I still have a look at stuff sometimes, if I'm alone in the house,' she said. 'Then I need to clear the browsing history, complete secret thing again. Even if I see something that appears to be fine, the question in my mind is, "Oh God, what if she catches me?" And that kind of kills the passion.' It reminds me of Zoe and what she said about the porn itself being directed towards shame. It makes sense of why we might try to hide it, but it doesn't make it easier when it's being hidden from us.

Finding out their secret

Lynne was in her fifties now, but when she was a kid her dad ran a second-hand tool shop and was always on the lookout for various odds and ends. On weekends in the early eighties, she'd go with him around various garages gathering spare parts and funny stories. She always noticed the Page Three topless models, she said, that were plastered on the walls next to the latest Pirelli calendars featuring naked and semi-naked women. And though at first she remembered feeling embarrassed, as she got a bit older it was different and she looked up to those women as being rightfully proud of their bodies. That was pretty much the extent of porn for her; she looked at a couple of magazines with her first husband but it never came to that much. It wasn't really until she married again a few years ago that porn came into her life, and it almost ended in divorce.

'I'd just had an operation,' she told me. 'I'd been having problems with my ovaries and adhesions and one thing and another, and we hadn't been particulary sexually active for a while because I was in a huge amount of pain. My husband was at work, I was at home, and I was starting to feel better but bored. So, I was on the computer thinking, "What shall I do?" and I noticed a folder that had the name of one of our favourite cartoon characters.' So, she clicked on it and found a folder called 'New Folder', which she thought must be the cartoons that he had just downloaded. She clicked on that and there it was:

her husband's porn collection. She said the bottom fell out of her world. 'It was a bit like when you're told that someone has died, that way time slows down and you can't really believe it,' she told me. 'There was nothing illegal there, it wasn't teenagers and stuff. It was more or less Page Three level of porn, naked women, that kind of thing. But, even so, there were a lot of images and it split us up basically because I felt that he had lied to me for the whole of our relationship. We'd been together about seven or eight years and whenever the issue of porn had been raised, he'd said, "Oh yes, it's revolting, people hiding in dark corners with these massive collections." And it's like, "Why did you lie to me about all of this?" I flicked through a few and then permanently deleted them off the system, called him at work and told him not to come home.' They ended up working it through in therapy and managed to stay together. But the betrayal cut deep, not just the porn but the lying, and it's not only something that's happened to Lynne.

Most sex and relationship experts will tell you that problems with one partner's porn use is a regular reason for couples coming into therapy these days; primarily, but not only, heterosexual couples and mostly, but not only, because of the porn practices of men. The approach to resolving this seems to differ both individually, obviously, depending on the circumstances of the couple, but also by the type of expert consulted, whether they specialize more in the area of sex or relationships. One who definitely errs on the side of the former is sexpert extraordinaire Dan Savage.

I lived in Vancouver in the early 2000s and one of my weekly highlights was reading his sex and relationships column in the free paper, the *Georgia Straight*. 'Savage Love' was – and still is – a wildly popular, internationally syndicated advice column where Dan Savage dishes out wisdom on everything from polyamory and sexting to gonorrhoea and how to broach a lover's less than ideal hygiene habits. While the internet has meant Savage has reached heights of infamy barely possible when I first encountered him, he has maintained the same sometimes brutal, often questionable, but overall highly entertaining approach to readers' questions about sex that made me a fan back in the day. With twenty more years of sexual experience under my belt, his columns now seem a bit more problematic; focused a little too much on individual choices and not enough on the social context that is both behind and bounds these. But his approach to taking the shame out of sex still feels incredibly needed. Particularly in the context where we're all finding it hard to tell anything other than the 'right kind' of sexual story.

One of his best-known responses was from 2012, regarding a reader's concern about her male partner's pornography habit. Having recently worked through the discovery that her boyfriend was cheating on her, the woman had then found out he'd been watching porn – though her partner didn't know about her discovery. Her question was whether this indicated he was more likely to cheat again. It seemed as if she wasn't so bothered by the porn, more by the ongoing deception, but Savage's response seemed to bypass this and instead lay out a simple equation. 'All men watch porn,' he said. 'Some lie and claim they don't, some are so stealthy they never get caught, but all men watch porn. So, we can safely say that porn viewing doesn't cause men to cheat. Because all men watch porn. But not all men cheat.'[7] Though he did allow a caveat that of course some tiny proportion of men might buck this general trend, his overall message was clear: men's porn use is inevitable and women's concern is irrational – or even hysterical, as, about four years later, he told another woman she needed therapy to accept that all men use porn. It's something that women are told regularly if we say men's use is a problem. It tells us to basically calm down and shut up, and the result is that we doubt ourselves.

Rachael was about a decade younger than Lynne but had a similar response to finding out about her partner's porn use. 'I started going out with my current partner about a year ago,' Rachael told me. 'We'd been friends for years before that. I'd read an article about some research from Australia about the effect of porn on teenagers. I mentioned it to him because he's got a teenage son and said, "You might need to talk to him about this." He said, "Oh yeah, but he's a boy, they're all going to be wanking over porn." So, I asked him if he did, and he said yes.' Rachael wasn't comfortable with that and she said so. 'On the one hand I've got this lofty intellectual argument about it, which is the whole thing that I think it does affect your brain and your other sexual interactions,' she told me. 'But on the other side of that, I have an emotional response to it. Women are trained from a really young age to be submissive in sex and to orient the whole experience around men's pleasure and a man's orgasm. That whole paradigm gets created at a really young age and I think that porn just feeds it.' It meant she didn't feel OK with her partner using porn; it felt like he was participating in something that was ultimately harmful to women. She told him so, and thought that was the end of that. Until she found out that it wasn't. 'We left it at that at that time,' she said. 'Then when I asked him about it about three months later, and said, "So, have you carried on using porn?" he said, "No." We got to earlier this year and I asked him again and he said, "Well, yeah, but not since we've been living together." I didn't believe him. When I got a chance, I checked his phone and found that not only had he done so since we moved in together, he'd done so the previous day. He still doesn't know that I know that. I've never in my whole life felt compelled to check someone's phone. I was so ashamed of myself that I couldn't bear to confront him over it.'

Rachael left it for a while after that, not really sure what to do. She didn't want to tell him she knew that he'd lied but the knowledge felt like a weight on her chest. Then the weekend just before we spoke it all came to a head. They'd been talking about sex or masturbation and he'd said he had a wank last week. So, Rachael asked if he'd used porn and he said no far too quickly. She didn't believe him as before, but he promised he was being truthful. She slept on it but still felt sick the next day so sat down with him and asked for his phone. 'He handed it over and he knew I was going to find it,' she said, 'so why wouldn't he just tell me? For him it was easier for me to check his internet history than for him to just say, "I did it, I've been lying to you."' Again, it was the deception more than anything else and a sense that her boundaries had been ignored completely. It wasn't only that he hadn't chosen to stop, but that he hadn't done so despite the knowledge it would hurt her.

I don't know where they got to in the end; when we spoke, it had only just happened. But the overwhelming feeling from Rachael at that time was that she was the one being forced to make a decision. 'We're in a slightly awkward situation now,' she told me. 'I've got to say, well, bugger off, or accept that he's going to watch porn and give him permission to do that. It's just uncomfortable for me, either scenario, isn't it?

Either way, I've got to swallow something huge – no pun intended.'

Whether or not Dan Savage – like Rachael's partner – is right and most men do use porn, that isn't really the point. It's the way that women are responded to for raising men's use as a problem – as though the problem lies with us. It feeds a broader cultural sense that women's view of the world isn't valid. And it also overlooks the research that suggests women might be onto something when they say it feels like an infidelity. In contrast to the studies on what porn can do for women in relationships – increasing our arousal, acting as a form of foreplay – it seems that porn can have the opposite impact for men in relationships with women. Although studies have reported findings which link female and couple pornography use with increased sexual desire and satisfaction respectively, men's solo pornography use within a relationship has been linked with a variety of negative effects, for both the men and the relationship. Effects such as increased relationship conflict, less female sexual desire, lower male positive communication and less overall relationship satisfaction. It also seems to have an impact

on our sex lives, and not just in terms of the practices men bring to the bedroom. A study from
2020 looking at over 200 mixed-sex and same-sex
couples found that while men in relationships
with other men who used porn alone and together
were more likely to have sex with their partner
on days that they had viewed porn, men in relationships with women were less likely to have sex
with their partners on the days that they use porn.
This is something supported by other studies
which find that heterosexual men's use of porn
improves their emotional wellbeing in the short
term but results in lower levels of sexual arousal,
fewer partnered sexual activities and, ultimately,
lower sexual wellbeing when looked at over time.[8]

Maybe some of this is what women are trying
to express when they talk about feeling that
watching porn is like cheating – a sense that it is
impacting their sex life because, in reality, it probably is. But women's discomfort is too readily
dismissed as invalid, coming from a place of
moral judgement and not a reasonable response.
It can lead to a sense of being divided; caught
between being bothered about what your partner
is doing and wanting to be the cool girl who just
doesn't care. In some ways both Rachael and
Lynne were protected from this; their ages meant

they had largely missed the mainstreaming of porn. But younger women talked about this conflict often and probably none more articulately than Laura.

Laura was a white woman who was almost thirty when we spoke and hadn't used porn much at all. But from an early boyfriend who first showed her porn at seventeen to what happened when she was dating the man who eventually became her husband, men's use of porn was definitely a relationship theme – and an ongoing point of tension. At seventeen Laura had asked her boyfriend if he could show her the porn he watched. She knew porn existed but had never actually seen it and was curious to know what it was all about. He went onto one of the mainstream sites and Laura was shocked by what she saw, something her boyfriend tried to quickly smooth over. 'It was fairly mainstream porn so obviously quite rough and not particularly intimate,' she told me. 'It was a man and a woman – I can't remember the exact position. I remember at the time my boyfriend specifically saying, "I don't want us to have sex like that, or you to look like that, I'm just watching it." But I also remember being horrified by it. I was upset that it wasn't the type of sex that we were having and they didn't look anything like me.'

A few years later it came up again with another boyfriend and this time Laura was angry, but not only at her partner. 'I took it as a personal affront that he would want to look at it,' she said. 'But then I was also really angry at myself for being bothered by it. I felt like it was a really normal part of young men's sexual lives and that I was just being jealous.' It was that pressure Maddie and Blair had spoken about – a sense you had to be sex positive even when you're not feeling that positive at all. It can encourage us to push down how we're feeling, creating that familiar sense that if there's something wrong, it must be with us. This mixed-up feeling continued when Laura met her husband. They watched porn together a few times early on but he never lasted that long when they had sex afterwards and she said it left her feeling like she was just somewhere to deposit. So they stopped sharing it but he kept using it and a few years later when they moved in together that started to cause a problem. 'I would really beat myself up that I was bothered by it, because again I felt like it was something that I should be OK with. I felt like I was being a jealous girl-friend because of it. Not necessarily from my partner but just in general,' she said. 'I wanted to be the type of person that was OK with porn. Who didn't take that as a personal slight or didn't feel insecure. I felt torn, like, "I'm feeling really upset but I should be cool with this." I was annoyed that I wasn't.' It ended up creating a lot of arguments. She didn't feel she could tell him she wasn't comfortable with his porn watching and he was half waiting for her to tell him to stop. In the end his use started waning because he could see how it was becoming such a source of tension, and Laura looked into the industry and felt more able to articulate her discomfort. 'As I got older and as I talked about it more with my friends, I got more aware of inequality and sexual violence and got more educated in my anger,' she said. 'And yes, I didn't like it personally because I didn't like my partner looking at other women in that way, but also, I had other views on it. I got more opinionated and then I felt OK in my anger. Like I don't like how women are being portrayed here, I don't like the messages this is sending. So then, because I was talking about that more just in a general sense, I think my partner absorbed it.' For Laura it was about moving from the personal to the political that seemed to make the difference. Shifting the problem from being about her own insecurity to being based on porn's treatment of women.

A few years older than Laura, Daisy had also felt the struggle of trying to make herself OK with what her partner was doing. 'You feel a bit prudish,' she told me. 'Like, "Don't be so frigid, men are into this." But also, like Laura, she could never sell herself on that completely and it's because what lay behind her discomfort was something deeper than a sense of competition or insecurity about her own sexual skills.

Daisy told me she'd only had two partners who she knew had watched porn. In the first relationship it didn't have any impact on their sex life, but in the most recent one it had left her feeling violated. She felt that sometimes it was as if her partner wasn't present during sex. 'It was like he had to go somewhere else to come,' she said. And like Clare, whose ex sent her off to go swinging, she experienced her partner bringing his porn use into their sex life, though she didn't know it at the time. When they first got together, Daisy told me, there were things that didn't make sense to her. 'He would come over my head, and in my face. I was thinking, "Where did you get that from?"' she said. At that point she didn't know about his porn use or what he was watching. But she soon found out and after that it all started making sense. 'I walked in on him watching porn late one night, and he wouldn't talk about it, he just shut the lid,' she said. 'So later I went onto his laptop to look at what he had, and there was this site called something like "facial abuse". I watched it and I just felt like I didn't know the person I was with any more.'

Daisy confronted her boyfriend about it and he was pretty shaken up. He didn't want to discuss it with her at all; he went quiet and completely shut down. So, Daisy searched online for information about the site and started sending him links about the women on it, how they didn't enjoy it and some were underage. But she could never get him to talk about it and over time the need to have the conversation just went away. In some ways, the damage was already done. 'I was just forever suspicious, and our relationship disintegrated really,' she said. 'There were times when I would check his laptop again, and I think he became very good at covering his tracks. It got to the point where I thought I can't just keep checking up on him. I had to let it go.' They stayed together for a few years afterwards but eventually broke up. Daisy said it wasn't only because of the porn; the trust had gone and it had taken the intimacy with it. She learned a lot from the experience about how porn was made and why she'd had such a reaction. 'When I first found out about my partner, it was something that I felt as a threat to me. It was the fact that often the girls are younger and very pretty. They have very nice bodies, so I did feel threatened,' she told me. 'But then I think, my learning curve has totally come from him, because it made me go out there and do my own research. And know that, no, I'm not a prude; some porn is all right but there's other porn that is horrible. It's something that's totally geared towards men, and quite violent, and discriminating against women. And I think, unfortunately, the internet is probably 80 per cent that kind. So, you know, I have just left him to it.' Like Rachel, Daisy was the one who ended up being forced to choose, not between her partner and porn, but between accepting his use or being alone.

For many women porn enters our lives through our most intimate relationships, sometimes without our knowledge. When it gets there, it can cause conflict or create connection; can bring us closer or drive us further apart. For most of the women I've spoken to, porn in relationships was a point of tension. Something to negotiate around, a source of secrecy and silence for their partners and themselves. It can feel like a betrayal – like cheating somehow – despite our attempts at playing it cool. Not just about jealousy but something more fundamental about how porn sees women and what that says about us. But for some, it played a part in making space for a conversation, about what we like sexually and what we want. And that's a space a lot of us need, even if porn's not the way that we get it.

VIOLENCE

Watching violence

As MUCH AS WE MIGHT not want it to be true, we know that some of the violence we see in porn is real. As did Myra, who'd said she couldn't watch porn with her partner any more after seeing a rape. And Violet, who'd told me that some of the aggressive porn she'd watched felt too hardcore in terms of abusing human rights and she'd had to turn it off. Acknowledging that some porn contains real violence isn't fear-mongering or hysteria, and ignoring it isn't helping. It's not the only industry with sexual violence built into its fabric; what we have seen with #MeToo proves that and, even then, what that exposed is undoubtedly the tip of the iceberg. But the difference is that, unlike Hollywood, the porn industry aims primarily to arouse us. That can leave us feeling complicit; wondering what happened to the women we've seen, as well as whether and how they got through it. A lot of women know from experience just how much sexual violence harms, and it's a harm that for some of us porn has been implicated in producing. This chapter wasn't easy to write, and it won't be easy to read. Accounts of violence are hard to hear, but they're still a part of our story.

For years, Pornhub prided itself on having the world's largest collection of pornography online, until an exposé by the *New York Times* in 2020 resulted in the removal of pretty much most of it. At the time, *VICE* reported that the number of videos displayed on the site's search bar dropped from 13.5 million to 4.7 million overnight as Pornhub removed all the content from unverified accounts, including the most viewed non-verified amateur video with apparently more than 29 million views.[1] The reason for this abrupt change, from the model of anyone uploading and downloading anything that had been the site's modus operandi – and a key reason for its success – since its beginnings in 2007, wasn't that company directors suddenly realized that this approach gave a green light for material to be shared and copied without accountability for its production or to its performers. Porn performers who were routinely having their copyrighted material distributed on the site without their permission had been campaigning for Pornhub to make a change like this almost since its inception. Nor was it really about what was in the *New York Times* exposé, a feature-length article which talked with survivors of child sexual abuse and trafficking who had videos of their abuse uploaded and reuploaded and had struggled for years to get them removed. As with performers, Pornhub had long been made aware that its platform was being used to circulate videos that were unlawful and that the ease with which anyone could set up an account was part of the problem. No, Pornhub didn't remove the content because it found out what the site was being used for. It did so because *we* found out what the site was being used for, as did Mastercard and Visa, which promptly suspended payments on the platform. It shows how important our attention is; sites like Pornhub do a lot to try to hold our attention online and seem to be able to make some radical changes if they're getting the wrong kind of attention offline. But while the removal of unverified uploads and claims of expanded moderation will undoubtedly make it harder for illegal and non-consensual content to be shared on Pornhub, it will do little to stop verified users uploading pornographic depictions of violence. This is porn which represents violence as something that is sexually arousing both for the men who are usually doing it and the women they're usually doing it to. From acts like hair pulling, slapping, choking – a lot of what has these days been called 'rough sex' – through to depictions of incest, abduction and rape. It's material that some women are shocked by and that others of us seek out, and whether or not it should stay on porn sites is the subject of quite heated debate; one I got pulled into a couple of years ago.

When I first started talking to women about porn, I realized fairly quickly that the evidence base on what porn actually is was limited, to say the least. It is hard for researchers to analyse the content that most of us watch online not only because there's just so much of it, but also because it moves so quickly. Videos can be uploaded, downloaded and deleted in the same day. It's a shifting target, which makes it difficult to pin down and study, at least in any way that is academically reliable. I'd heard the claims that over the last decade porn had become more hardcore; that it was more body-punishing, more aggressive, more violent than it used to be. But finding valid research to back this up is difficult because there's nothing that has established a baseline: we don't know if things are getting worse because we don't know where we're starting from. So, in 2017, my colleagues at Durham University and I ran a study designed to track the content of mainstream online pornography.[2]

We developed a way of accessing the front page of the UK's three most popular websites every hour without them knowing that we were the same computer. This meant we were able to see what they advertise to a first-time, anonymous user; what content their data tells them will keep that user scrolling. We wanted to establish a baseline so in ten, twenty, thirty years' time the researchers that come after us can tell us what has changed. For now, we've got a fairly good measure of what the big sites are trying to sell us, and it turns out it's a whole lot of violence against women. Over a period of six months, we found over 12,000 videos on the front page of these sites describing acts of sexual violence. It's not that these videos were of actual violence, though of course some of them likely were. But they were videos based on the idea that being violent is sexually arousing for men, and experiencing violence is sexually arousing for women. And they were being shown to every one of those 120 million daily users, the moment that they clicked on the site. When we published the study early in 2021 it made international headlines. This time, however, Pornhub doubled down just as they did when called out about racist porn. The company line is all about tapping into a long-standing debate about whether porn is just fantasy. 'Consenting adults are entitled to their own sexual preferences as long as they are legal and consensual. All kinks that meet these criteria are welcome on Pornhub,' a spokesperson said. Leaving to one side the fact that's simply untrue – Pornhub, XVideos and Xhamster (which were the two other sites we looked at) all had terms and conditions that were explicitly against the vast majority of what we found – Pornhub's response treads well-worn ground in the debates about violence in porn.

While there is widespread agreement that when porn is a record of violence it shouldn't be available for anyone, this gets a bit more complicated when we're talking about representations. This is the claim that porn is just fantasy, and so attempts to limit the violence that we see in porn become an attempt to limit the sexual fantasies – and freedom – of those who might want to see it. But the relationship between porn and fantasy is more complicated than that. Porn isn't just in our sexual imagination, even if that's where it ends up. It's a record of something that happened; the people are real and so is the sex. It's also a product produced for profit, the vast majority of which goes nowhere near the actors. However, hiding this reality under the appeal to porn as fantasy is a really useful strategy for mainstream porn sites. It means that any criticism of the content they're choosing to platform – what's in it, how's it made, or how it got on the site in the first place – becomes a criticism of what users are choosing to view and their freedom to fantasize in the privacy of their own homes. From corporate responsibility to individual agency, it's a clever sleight of hand.

Once concerns about violence in pornography are reduced to being judgements of the individuals who watch it, the porn sites themselves are off the hook. But far from what companies such as Pornhub might want us to believe, people with 'kinks that meet these criteria' can also have a problem with what's available online. Maybe a lot more than we've been led to believe.

When Harper was just hitting her teenage years, she began watching hardcore sado-masochistic porn. This continued right through until her mid-twenties, when we spoke. Her story makes us question simple narratives of escalation. Because it's not that she eased into using this kind of material – it was literally her starting point.

It began at thirteen with an article she found in *Cosmopolitan*. It talked about erotica for women, its usefulness and where to find it, and included among other things the web address of one particular platform. She went straight to her family desktop computer, waited until no one was watching, and printed out a bunch of stories about bondage, domination and rape. Turns out, that was the site's main focus. Not long after, her mother came across what she'd printed and asked her what the hell was going on. Harper lied and said the boys at school had given them to her, something that – luckily – her mum never followed up on. At that point Harper stopped for a while; she told me she felt guilty about what she'd read and about blaming the boys. But then a few months later she was back online, and this time she found those free torrent sites that were popular when I was young and allowed for peer-to-peer file sharing. 'A few months after my mum spoke to me, I started downloading porn,' she said. 'Some really weird stuff as well. I was downloading this forced incest thing and another couple of ones that were BDSM and quite rapey. I don't actually remember looking at anything that wasn't like that really.'

Over the next few years, Harper got better at hiding what she was doing and better at finding what she wanted. But that early sense of guilt was never far away, particularly because of what she was watching. It was something she'd thought a lot about, why it was she was so drawn to that kind of porn. She thought some of it might have to do with her own experiences of violence, but she was never quite sure. 'It's hard because I was in a very abusive relationship when I was about fifteen and after that I've had various sexual assaults and things, so violence is very much a personal experience I've had,' she said. 'But at the same time, throughout all of that and even before I was in a violent relationship, I've always found women being beaten and treated very aggressively arousing.' She told me that she used to be very into rape porn, particularly of women when they were asleep. And also said she was sexually assaulted herself once when sleeping. She wasn't sure how connected those two things were. It was about that conflict again, between our pleasure and our principles, the borderline. And it was something that Harper found hard to resolve and so she just lived with the tension. 'It's taken me a long time to work through it and I don't think I ever actually have managed to do that,' she said. 'Sometimes I think it brings me pleasure and that's good enough and feminist, but I'm someone who's very passionate about violence against women and then really into very violent pornography. It upsets me because I don't know why it turns me on. It's difficult to reconcile, I think.'

The question of how pornography is implicated in violence against women is still largely un-answered. Some believe that pornography is the cause of violence and the attitudes that underpin it, though this gets more complicated when we acknowledge how many women are watching porn, and not the soft, fluffy kind either. For others, it's a form of violence itself; we know that some women in porn are assaulted on screen, for example, while other women have their assaults uploaded. Then there's the argument that there is no real connection: that porn is just a representation and there's no real-world impact beyond that. Given how different these claims are, there's been a great deal of research trying to work out which one holds more weight.

Studies that look at the relationship between watching porn and accepting violence seem to suggest the two are connected. When the bulk of effects-based studies are analysed together, researchers find a correlation between watching violent pornography and attitudes that condone violence against women.[3] But it's not necessarily a 'monkey see, monkey do' situation. Researchers aren't sure if what they're seeing is that people who already have these kinds of attitudes seek out violent porn (the beliefs shaping the porn), or that watching violent porn increases someone's acceptance of violence more broadly (the porn shaping the beliefs). In some ways it's an impossible thing to measure; there's no way to isolate porn from all other influences and these days it would be hard to find a control group that hasn't seen at least some violent porn, given its ubiquity on the front pages of the biggest porn sites. But the other thing to know here is that the research showing a relationship between watching violence in porn and condoning it has been conducted almost entirely on men alone. This means that we don't know what, if any, relationship exists there for women. And that's important because it seems as though the usual explanations just don't fit.

When we spoke, River was just coming out of what she called a heavy porn habit. Unlike Harper's fairly immediate use of porn showing violence against women, for River it seemed to happen more slowly. 'I remember reading things when I was younger that would say, "In order to enhance your sex life, get a porn film, and watch it together." So, I thought, "Right, well, I am going to have a really good sex life with my partner, so let's get a porno, and have a kinky night,"' she told me. 'It was with my first partner, but it was through a cadet's military environment. I was young and he was eight years older than me. I wanted to be "the cool girlfriend" that accepted this kind of stuff. "Watch it, copy it, join in with it", you know.'

From watching it with him, it turned into a private practice, and one that taught her about sex and her sexual role. Over time what she watched became more explicit, until she was actively seeking out porn that showed women being humiliated. 'I took great pride in copying things like deep-throating,' she said. 'And learned how to get off on the idea of guys having power over me. I used to watch guys training women. Women pleasing their "master". I hate that I did this, but I used to get off to that.' Porn started to shape her sexual behaviour; like Eleanor had said, she felt it had 'wound its way' in. She came to believe her role was to give men pleasure. She said she learned to be aroused by violence. 'I went through a stage which I now don't enjoy, of things that are normalized by the category "the rape fantasy",' she told me. 'I learned to masturbate to this stuff which all became very violent. I learned to take violence. I learned to behave.'

When most of this was going on, River was in the military, deployed in a country with few connections and little space to be herself. Looking back on it now, she thought the similarities between that and porn compounded the impact. Together they left her feeling dehumanized; not an individual with emotions, just an object that had to obey. 'If you have been in the military, because you are dehumanized in that way, then it is very easy to copy and train that kind of stuff,' she said. 'Being a soldier had got me to the point where I couldn't think for myself. I could function, I could go to work. But then I would come home and put porn on. I was like a feral fox, hiding away.'

In her mid-twenties River left the military but the porn habit came with her. It stayed for a few years until one day, unprompted, she decided to tell an old family friend. She was someone River looked up to, who she felt had a sense of the bigger picture, and it meant that River trusted her enough to talk about what she was doing. After a particularly open conversation, this friend sent River a TED Talk about one man's decision to stop using porn. It was gentle, not judgemental, a nudge and not a push. And for River it was a new experience of being treated like a person with choices. She started looking for information about the porn industry and interrogating how it made her feel. She realized she wasn't happy with what she was doing and so began the process of weaning herself off it. 'As soon as I knew that I could do different things, that's when I managed to break the relationship with it,' she said. 'It was just small steps at first and then basically, one day, I decided I'm not going to do it again. And after that, I haven't.'

For River and Harper, watching violent porn didn't correlate neatly with condoning violence against women; there was something more complicated going on. They didn't feel women deserved to be treated badly, even if – as River said explicitly – they'd come to believe that for themselves. It was true across the women I spoke to, who talked about watching violence in porn. They wanted to know the women were OK, even if they were aroused by the idea of them experiencing violence. Some didn't know why it aroused them; like Harper, it was a source of confusion and conflict. But others did have a sense of what it was, and it wasn't as easy as believing that it's OK to hurt women. Sometimes it was about authenticity and feeling like you were watching a real response. Like Prena, who'd said she needed a hint of non-consensualness, and told me there was something you got from seeing pain that was different to watching someone fake pleasure. 'I think one of the reasons that I seek out painful or too rough porn is because I want to hear a noise that is genuine,' she said. 'I just want something real and often you'll only hear real noises if it's too rough, which is a horrible thought actually.' For other women, it was the opposite; it was much more about escape. Vanessa, who'd talked about watching 'fucked-up stuff' – the interracial porn that threw up ads for videos of the

KKK – said her arousal was based on the pretence of it. 'Quite a lot of what I enjoy, I know enough about how bodies work to be able to say I don't think it would be pleasurable,' she told me. 'But there's a fantasy there that it would be mind-blowing. That's what I'm interested in. I don't go to porn for the reality of the sex.' For Sophia, it was something else, something in between; she wanted the realness in the performance. It was about hearing people talk about what they were going to do, and then watching their fantasies play out. And she found all that on a site called Kink.com.

At thirty now, Sophia used to be very comfortable with her porn use. She spoke to her friends about it openly – particularly those who still felt unsure even talking about masturbation – and didn't really have the tension that so many of the other women who talked to me seemed to have. She mostly watched BDSM and, like Harper, spoke about using Kink.com, a paid-for fetish site whose popularity, in part, is due to providing filmed shorts that tell the story of the production. This includes interviews with the actors before and after filming which, given the often physically intense nature of what is depicted, can be used by the audience to verify that everyone they watched wanted everything that happened. For Sophia, these trailers were part of the pleasure. 'I think what turns me on the most in the movies isn't just the brutality of the so-called "rape" scenes,' she said. 'It's the ten-minute video at the beginning and at the end, where you see the girl being talked through the scene and she talks about how she's excited about it and wants to try this and wants to try that. Then afterwards it's the girl being interviewed again and she says, "That was great. I've always wanted to be tied up by my feet or whatever."' These interviews worked to help Sophia trust the content, which in turn helped allay any sense of unease about what it was she was watching. But even with checks and balances in place things can go wrong. That happened both for Kink.com and for Sophia.

In 2015, Stoya — a well-known 'alt porn' actress — said she had been raped by her former boyfriend, one of the site's most popular male performers, James Deen. This was followed by eight different women disclosing sexual and physical assaults by him, occurring both on set and off. Deen has denied these claims, as well as those by Stoya, but it's also come out that — like Harvey Weinstein — Deen was known by some in the industry as a man who 'doesn't like limits', and the similarities don't end there. A 2020 article in *Cosmopolitan* described the incident as being the #MeToo of the porn industry and questioned why it hadn't been taken seriously, with Deen's career mostly unaffected while some of the women involved have been ridiculed on set and found it hard to get work. The same article included an interview with a woman using a pseudonym who had been a star of the porn industry for years.[4] She spoke about being assaulted on the set of an unnamed production company and then asked to film an exit interview like the ones Sophia watched, in which she said everything was consensual. 'I was so desperate to get out of there,' she told the interviewer. 'I was in shock, I was afraid. I thought, "If he wants me to say yes to everything then that's what I'm going to do."' Which, though thinking about it like that makes complete sense, effectively renders those interviews pointless.

While the *Cosmo* article voiced the concerns of porn performers who'd worked for a range of producers, it left out claims made about the production company of Erika Lust – the independent feminist pornography creator that the magazine regularly encourages women to check out. The non-binary Black performer Rooster has said they experienced unethical and abusive behaviour by the female porn director and actor Olympe de G on a Lust shoot, including that a sexual assault was filmed and is part of Lust's movie *Architecture Porn*, a claim that Olympe de G denies. Lust also denied it initially, refusing that the claims amounted to assault, though later she removed the film from her website and issued a joint statement with Rooster where both acknowledged and apologized for any harm done to the other. It looks like even in feminist porn there can be people with unethical behaviour. And even when producers are trying to get things right, there are no guarantees of safety for performers.[5]

For Sophia, though, it actually wasn't the James Deen scandal that ended her willingness to believe everyone was all right. That happened when she saw what she thought was a real rape a few years before porn's #MeToo moment. 'In 2011, I found a video on a particular site which presented itself as one of those fake taxi films, and when I opened it, it turned out to be a snuff movie of a very real Japanese woman with someone intruding into her house and raping her,' she told me. She said there was no button to report it, nothing she could do, and that any time she'd tried to talk about it she had been told that it wasn't real. 'I told a couple of people about it, but they'd always come back and say, "No, no, it's a genre." I went, "No, these were real tears." I know the difference because I like kink, I like to see someone who is willingly getting hit or tied up. There's a difference between "I'm crying but I'm clearly enjoying this" and uncontrollable sobs of "This is happening to me and now my life is ruined."'

Sophia said what she saw was a wake-up call that changed how she felt about porn. Where before she talked about her use as gleeful – she didn't care what she watched, would download from wherever – after that it all felt wrong. It became something private again, used less and more warily. 'It was really traumatic,' she said. 'I closed the window, and I couldn't look at porn at all for about six months. I've withdrawn from anything now where there isn't a valid system of reporting because I couldn't help that woman. She's somewhere in the world – this happened to her and I saw it. And I was powerless to help.'

Experiencing violence

The conversation with Lubna was one of the hardest that I had. So hard in fact that I was contacted by the woman who was transcribing the interviews to say how much she'd been affected and to ask how Lubna was doing, such is the kindness of women towards each other. Lubna was doing OK, she was doing better than OK. She was an incredible mother and grandmother, the kind that I want to be. She was a company director and business graduate whose second husband saw the beautiful woman she was and treated her accordingly. She was and is a whole person who is so much more than what was done to her by someone who found that wholeness threatening. But still, she has to carry it.

Lubna was in her sixties when we spoke, Asian and Muslim, all things that she felt made it impossible for her to talk about not only the sexual violence she experienced from her ex-husband but also the kinds of material he was watching to help him do it. She told me that you are judged in particular ways for being abused as a South-East Asian woman, that 'even if the community has sympathy with the fact that you've suffered violence and abuse, you are still judged as having failed'. She thought this meant I would struggle to find women with backgrounds like hers who would talk to me. It turned out she was right, which makes what she told me all the more powerful, and her act of speaking it an act of resistance.

Lubna married her first husband when she was just eighteen and he was almost forty, after it was arranged by their parents. She knew that sex would be expected straight away but didn't know anything about it. 'I remember asking my mum because I was really frightened,' she said. 'I was born and brought up in the UK so I'd gone to biology lessons where they tell you the mechanics but that's all I knew. And my mum was really embarrassed – as I would be if my children were asking me about sex – and said, "I'll get your aunty to speak to you." Which she did but all my aunt said to me was, "It will be painful for the first few times but after that it'll be OK." That was it, that was all I was told.' On her wedding night the first thing her husband said to her was that she was his wife now and that meant he expected her to do as he said. Never to question him, to obey him and his family, and never to cross the line. He then wanted to have sex with her and it hurt like hell so she started crying. He slapped her and held his hand over her mouth. She told me she thought that night she would die. It continued for a few more nights until it started getting less painful.

A few months later and she'd moved away from her family to London and started sorting out the flat they were living in, sharing with his brother and cousin. There was a big cupboard in the hallway which she started cleaning out and it was there that she found his porn stash. 'When I say stash, there must have been about thirty videos,' she said. 'VHS cassettes and photographs. As I was cleaning, his cousin came in and asked what I was doing. I asked him whose photographs they were. He just said, "Ask your husband."' She didn't ask him that night, though, as she wanted to do some more digging. So, the next day she went back to the cupboard, collected all the photographs and put on one of the videos. She couldn't believe what she was seeing and she told her husband as soon as he got home. 'I said, "I've looked at the videos and they're disgusting." I took a beating for that. He said, "This is what men do. You've got no problems. My friends will come over. If we decide to watch videos, we're watching videos. You are to stay in your room.

You're not to tell anyone. Don't you dare question me." So that was that.'

From that point on his violence got worse. He started to force Lubna to give him oral sex, and if she refused, he beat her. She had three miscarriages because of the beatings. He raped her anally three times; one time she bit him so hard fighting him off that she drew blood and he threatened to have her arrested. She didn't think porn was the reason he was violent, that was too much of an excuse. But she knew from experience that it was being used as validation; a justification for what he was doing to her. 'I remember him beating me,' she said. 'And I was just lying on the floor and he kept telling me not to move, not to move, and then he ejaculated all over me. He did that countless times. I remembered seeing a guy ejaculating over a woman on the video of his I watched. He would refer back to those videos. "I'll show you," he'd say, "what these women do to make their men happy."'

Lubna had no support and no resources to leave, but somehow, one day, she did. It wasn't enough to be free of his violence. She remembers walking home with the kids from school; they'd been free for a few months, the sun was shining, and he was standing at the front door of the house they had moved to. She had no option but to let him in. 'The kids ran to him, they were like "Daddy! Daddy!" There was nothing I could do,' she said. 'He stayed for a week and it was horrific. He raped me, tried to strangle me during sex. Then one morning he got up and he said to the children, "I've just got to go away for some work." He pulled the phone out of the wall and then he just went. I found out about six weeks later I was pregnant and I had to go for a termination.' She told me that her mother had never forgiven her for that and had told her the sin was on them all. When she left, Lubna was ostracized from her community; they thought her taking away his children was worse than what he was doing to her. But after he'd come back that time, she knew if he came again she wouldn't survive it. So, without any support from family or friends, Lubna got a solicitor. They got an injunction, pushed through the divorce, and though it meant starting from nothing, she got herself and her children free.

Porn gave legitimacy to Lubna's ex-husband's actions; it was something Derrington talked to me about, as porn being a way of *allowing* violence. She too had lived through the violence of an ex-partner, of two in fact, and saw porn as giving permission, not just to them but to others, to use violence against women with impunity. This isn't the same as a causal argument, that porn makes these men violent. Nor is porn being positioned as an excuse or encouragement; in some ways it's more concerning than that. Men like Lubna's ex-husband drew on porn as a form of inspiration. He took tips, ideas, used it like a blueprint. And he's not the only man to have done that.

That Joy chose to speak under the name Joy says a lot about where she's got to. Joy was a white Christian woman in her early thirties who spoke a lot about her faith. She told me that porn was a sin in the Christian community not so much because of its content but because of its connection to adultery. 'In the Christian faith there is an understanding that pornography is wrong,' she said. 'But the fundamental reason that pornography is wrong is that in the Bible there's a teaching where Jesus says even if you lust after somebody, you are committing adultery. Even just in your head, it's adultery. So that's how pornography is viewed.'

Joy was seventeen and a self-described

vulnerable teenager when she met her ex-
husband. She'd been sexually abused by a
neighbour for eight years as a child, and her parents had been extremely strict – she didn't even
have a TV growing up – meaning that she was
out of step with most kids her age. When she met
her ex she told him she was not going to have sex
before marriage. She was a devoted Christian
who loved Jesus and didn't want to disappoint
her family. Within twelve days he had manipu-
lated her into sleeping with him without
contraception and within six months she was
pregnant. They were married and stayed together
for the next four years, during which time he
became increasingly abusive. 'In some ways it's
really blurry,' she said. 'It's not like there are individual incidents, it was just four years of consistent
sexual violence in some form or another.' Within
four months of them getting together he had
coerced her into anal sex, which was painful and
unwanted. He signed them up for swinging websites, bullied her into threesomes and posted her
naked photos online – she felt dread to this day
knowing they were out there somewhere. He
raped her when she was pregnant – which she
was at eighteen and then again when she was
twenty. He urinated on her during sex and tried

to defecate on her after seeing it in a movie, though that was the one thing she was able to stop.

Like the man who abused Lubna, the man who abused Joy used porn to validate what he was doing. She couldn't remember exactly when it started, but early on he introduced it. He was heavily into file sharing, BitTorrents in the early 2000s. Joy said that he must have had thousands of videos which he'd make sure they watched together to normalize what he wanted her to do. 'The pornography meant that I didn't have a get-out because I couldn't say, "Well, people don't do that,"' she told me, but it wasn't only the porn that she felt had put her in that position. 'I'd had no healthy upbringing around sexuality or ownership of my own body,' she said. 'You just literally try to avoid thinking about sex and don't engage with your own body as a sexual thing. It meant that everything that he brought into the relationship in terms of pornography, I felt that I should see as normal. I should want to do it, and if I didn't it was just about my moral background. It wasn't that I had a right not to like this.'

Joy's second child was born three months

premature. As hard as that was, for the first time as an adult Joy was away from her ex-husband living in a hospital with her toddler and baby about an hour from their home town. It meant she got some space from him, some space to think, some space for action. It also meant that she found out he was having a relationship with a fourteen-year-old girl. 'By the age of nineteen he'd been a registered sex offender for having sex with under-age girls. When we were living in hospital, I found out he was still having a relationship with one of them,' she said. 'I'd gone home to pick up some clothes and she was hiding in the house somewhere. My dad was there and I couldn't bring myself to find her because if he saw her, he'd call the police and I'd just given birth to a baby.' Joy separated from her ex-husband after that, and when we spoke it was ten years later. She'd married again, this time to a lovely man she'd met through the Church, and had built back a relationship with God which didn't require her to deny her sexuality in the way she'd been taught as a child. The legacy of the abuse was something she carried with her but she'd been able to craft a beautiful life for herself and for her children despite it.

*

The experiences of Lubna and Joy, of porn being used to justify violence, are unique to them, but they aren't uncommon. It was something that came up for quite a few women I spoke with; the violence wasn't only in adulthood and wasn't only perpetrated by men. Coming of age in the sexually liberated seventies, Stacey told me the fear of sexual violence hung over her like a weight. She was petrified for years of being labelled loose because she felt it meant you were fair game. 'Growing up,' she said, 'this is the absolute truth, I was told that there's no such thing as rape because a man can't run with his trousers down but a girl can run with her skirt up.' These days, she didn't think much had changed but she also looked back at her childhood and saw there was something else in it that had scared her. Stacey was sexually abused as a child by someone she knew. And the first time she remembered seeing pornography was when a magazine was used in that abuse. 'The person abusing me was looking at it and getting me to replicate the pictures. I had to copy the pictures in the magazine,' she said. 'And then the pornography went on to include bestiality, which I was then subjected to as well.' Sara was also abused as a child, by her female babysitter when she was five. When we spoke it was forty years later, and the impact of that abuse was a big part of what she wanted to say. The babysitter used the threat of revealing that Sara had seen her father's porn stash as a way of making her stay quiet while she did to her what was in them. 'She said to me, "I've seen you looking at your dad's magazines"; it was just "I know you've been doing it", and a threat of telling my parents, and then she took me to my mum and dad's room. I think I'd only just started primary school.' Porn was used to make her feel complicit, as though what happened was her fault and not a choice made by someone else. It meant that for years porn was wrapped up with guilt, a lot of shame and the fear she felt being abused as a child.

When these experiences are taken together it becomes impossible to ignore that sometimes porn is used in sexual violence, as a resource for perpetrators and inspiration for what they do. It's something even the American serial killer Ted Bundy noted – that the violent men he'd met in prison all shared, like him, a deep involvement with porn. We've seen it recently worldwide with some high-profile cases: in the UK a serving police officer who abducted, raped and killed a woman he didn't know – thirty-three-year-old Sarah

Everard – was also a regular user of what was described during his trial as 'violent sexual pornography'. In Aotearoa, New Zealand, the man who raped and murdered Grace Millane, a twenty-two year old British woman he'd met through Tinder, had searched online for porn of people defecating on women just minutes after he'd killed her.[6] We know porn plays a role here and these cases aren't unique, and yet there's actually not that much research exploring how porn is used by perpetrators of domestic and sexual violence.

While researchers spend a fair amount of time trying to track how porn influences attitudes and behaviours among the general population, there's been less of a focus on how it has been used by perpetrators. The research that has been done seems to suggest that men who rate highly on scales for things like beliefs in traditional gender roles and self-reported likelihood of using sexual aggression interpret and react to pornography in particular ways; that they read it as a legitimation of their personal desires and attitudes. Thinking back to that 3AM model of sexual socialization, it is not that men who use violence only acquired the script that violence is sexually arousing through watching violent pornography. It's more that this script is activated – and reinforced – by porn depicting violence and that encourages them to apply what they see, particularly when so much of the language around women on the mainstream sites depicts us as being there for men's pleasure. In effect, it's not that porn is making all men violent, but for those who want to be it is making it easier. This is similar to what Lubna and Joy are saying. It's not that their husbands became violent because of porn, that's too causal, too much of an excuse. But they used it as a resource for what they wanted to do, a handy tool in their toolbox.

Surviving violence

There is another place where porn, violence and women collide and it's not something I'd ever really considered until women started to say it. Porn might have a role in helping us come back to ourselves in the aftermath of sexual violence. The hope here is that the right porn at the right time might help women who've experienced violence to feel ownership over our bodies and reclaim our sexual desire. No one's sure if it works but some of us are trying.

*

Sorrel – whose mum told her not to talk about her munchie – grew up in the pre-internet era, but porn was still the first time she learned about her body. At ten, Sorrel, her sister and one of her brother's girlfriends were looking in her brother's room and found a porn magazine under his pillow. It had images of women, and of men and women having sex, alongside little stories about who they were and what they liked doing. She recalls feeling initially curious and then some kind of arousal, but her brother's girlfriend said it's something for men and put the magazine away. 'I can't remember what the comment was but it was something like "only men look at these things",' she told me. 'I think if I had found the magazine by myself, I would have just looked at it, felt the arousal, and moved on. But I remember feeling this sense of shame thinking that I shouldn't feel like this, because this is what boys do.' Like Makeda, who'd gone upstairs to find her cousins watching porn, that message came early. It's not just porn that's not for girls and women. Sexual desire isn't either. Sorrel pretended not to be bothered, then snuck back in for the next few months to look at the porn alone. She told me it was how she came to grips with her body; how she explored what she looked like and learned what felt good. It was an experience with herself that she needed, because she'd never had the chance to feel like her body was hers.

Sorrel was sexually abused when she was younger; it began when she was three. She felt the abuse had marked her as 'bad' even as a toddler, so it meant that when she found her brother's magazines and they made her want to touch herself, she knew on the one hand that she shouldn't but on the other she felt like it didn't matter. 'I have a history of abuse so for me masturbation was somehow tied up with that history. It was almost like I was already classed as bad so it wasn't a bad thing,' she said. 'I knew anything to do with sex was bad but I had already been outed as this bad child who is sleeping with men so I just thought, well, I'm going to do it anyway because I like the feeling.' And so, she masturbated to porn from the age of ten, sneaking back into her brother's room regularly, and then later her mum's when she found she also had a stash. She said she looks back on it as an adult and nothing matches up. 'Going through it was so phenomenal; I had the best time with my own body,' she told me. 'I've never really had that same experience again, like nothing else can touch it.' She never understood why, until she went to counselling and talked it through. 'When I started therapy, I think it made it easier for me to articulate the messy bit about abuse that most people find difficult to explain,' she said. 'That one of the things that's so tough about it can be the physical pleasure you experience, even though you know it's abuse.'

The physical response that we can have to an experience of sexual violence is rarely discussed because of how it can be used to minimize the harm. We're so used to conflating arousal with pleasure that the whole thing can feel like it's a contradiction. But bodies are bodies and when they're touched in certain ways they respond; sometimes it's even about protection – lubrication, for example, to help lessen the likelihood of damage. This isn't arousal as we know it but, at the time, we don't know that. It feels like our bodies are betraying us.[7] This can be a huge source of silence and struggle and shame. For Sorrel, porn gave her a way out. Looking at the magazines and using them to masturbate put her back in the driver's seat. She didn't feel guilty – after all, she was already 'bad' – but it was a way to take back control of how her body responded. 'I don't know how to explain it,' she told me. 'When you're masturbating you have the same feeling you had in some ways to when the abuse was taking place. But somehow for me it was like I was taking back that pleasure. I was taking back my pleasure and it was on my terms.'

The role that porn might play in helping women in the aftermath of sexual violence is rightly a delicate subject. It's also something that's not often explored, particularly because of what we know is in most mainstream porn. But there's been a couple of key exceptions to this, and probably the most important one in the UK is the My Body Back Project. Created by the activist and midwife Pavan Amara, the My Body Back Project started out in 2014 as a website where those who had experienced sexual violence could discuss their difficulties with healthcare professionals and sex therapists and find places to seek support. Just two years later, Amara and the project had established the UK's first sexual health and maternity clinic in London specifically for survivors, with another clinic in Glasgow coming just two years later. Both clinics specialize in providing a space where anyone who has experienced sexual violence can access cervical screening, STI testing, and contraceptive and maternity care in a sensitive and supportive environment. They offer

longer appointments, specialist healthcare work-
ers and put no pressure on anybody to have any
kind of invasive tests before they feel ready.

Amara was raped as a teenager, something she's
spoken about publicly, and it was her own experiences in trying to find health professionals who
understood what she might be going through that
inspired the project's creation. Writing in the
Telegraph in 2017, she said that for years following the rape she'd felt unsafe in her body and that
had made even going for a check-up with her GP
difficult. After talking with other women when
she was a student nurse, she found she wasn't
alone in this and soon afterwards she started the
project. It quickly expanded from a focus just on
gynaecological care to include broader sexual
health in recognition of the impact of rape on
women's sex lives. It's part of the harms of sexual
violence that we don't talk about enough. The
way that it can steal one of our most intimate
relationships: the one that we have with our own
sexual pleasure. In 2016 – working with the
London-based women's sex shop Sh! – the My
Body Back Project set up Café V, a monthly
group session with tea and cakes focused on
enjoying sex, masturbation and your body after
surviving violence. The project also established

the Clit List, an online list of resources for people who wanted to explore their sexuality using feminist, non-misogynistic and empowering content. Speaking about it to *VICE*, Amara said the idea came after porn kept being brought up, both at the Café V sessions and at other workshops where she'd talk about My Body Back. 'Women wanted to be able to explore their sexuality in a safe way,' she said. 'But what ended up happening is that they'd try and do that with porn, and they'd just come across misogynistic, violent, horrible stuff that replicated what had happened to them, or showed rape as though it were normal. I thought, this is obviously a problem we should do something about, so we created a list of porn that women can safely watch – with no violence – that won't make us feel degraded.'[8] Though the Clit List seems to be offline now, when it was up and running you'd find things like written and visual porn (with free access provided by producers and sometimes through less ethical links to what should be paid-for content provided without paywalls on Pornhub), sex toy reviews, and a practical section with tutorials and advice. The porn had been carefully chosen by volunteers at the project, and it came complete with a description that helped you know what to expect. If only for breaking the long-standing taboo on talking about sex and pleasure after sexual violence, I'm sure the Clit List was valued by many women who used it. One of whom was Nell.

Nell told me she'd masturbated since she was borderline teen – she couldn't even remember how young – but even though it hurt like hell the first time a boy fingered her, she couldn't tell him he was doing it wrong. 'I should have compared what he did to what I did to myself and realized that you can ask for what feels good, that you know what feels good, because you've touched your own body,' she said. 'But it was almost like I didn't think of masturbation as a real form of sex or pleasure. Sexuality was only something I could access through someone else, what I did to myself didn't count.' It seems that the silence surrounding the realities of women's masturbation creates a sense of whose pleasure is legitimate, and who our bodies are for.

When I met Nell, in her mid-twenties, she was facing a different kind of struggle. Just before she went to university she was raped, and it was something that had consequences yet again for the pleasure that she was able to have with her body. When she was younger, Nell had briefly gone online to see what porn was all about. She was horrified at what she found and had never got past the thumbnails but she'd never really needed to – she said she had a good imagination. But fantasizing by herself had become much more difficult now. She didn't want to make things up herself, because being in her head wasn't the best place to be. 'After being raped, I need something to respond to, like an actual thing,' she told me. 'I need something to focus on that enables me not to turn into my own head. I can't just masturbate with nothing.' Enter Pavan Amara.

Nell told me that in the last couple of years she'd used the My Body Back Project and through that had found the Clit List. She said it was probably the most in touch she'd ever been with people directly saying it's good for women to masturbate. That in itself had been helpful, as well as the fact that she could read a description about what something was before seeing it. It was also the basic fact that someone had made the list to help with an impact of rape that's so unspoken. It helped her feel less alone, like she wasn't the only one struggling. But when you got down to the nitty gritty of what was being suggested, it just wasn't what she wanted. 'I looked at some of the stuff on it recently, like a couple of months ago, and it all just feels empty,' she said. 'It's like the possibility of exploitation was always lingering at the back of my mind and the fear it might descend into something that I didn't see coming. Even with one of the things that I watched I was just like, "This is awful, I can't believe it's recommended."' What feels OK and helpful for some of us might not feel the same for all of us. It makes it hard to have a list of suggestions, no matter how carefully chosen.

Marie seemed to have had a similar experience. Marie was a white woman who was approaching her twenty-fifth birthday the week that we spoke. She'd first seen porn with an ex-boyfriend when she was an undergraduate at Cambridge. It wasn't something she'd sought out herself, despite the fact that at twenty-four she could have had fairly easy access. But her ex wanted to watch it with her and wanted them both to masturbate. At the time Marie wasn't that into it but felt like she had to because it was what he wanted. 'That was how my sexual relationships were for a long time,' she said. 'I very much just went along with whatever my particular boyfriend wanted to do.

I didn't enjoy it, it made me uncomfortable but I got curious too and started watching it alone. It was a strange kind of education which I've thought about a lot since.'

Marie told me that porn filled the gaps left over from school; that it became a kind of default sex ed because what she was taught formally had been so lacking. She told me that though she'd been sexually active from thirteen she used to have trouble orgasming. Or more accurately, she never orgasmed with the boys she was with, and she'd never actually tried to do it herself, until porn. 'That's probably mostly what I learned; I used it to teach myself how to get off,' she said. 'I'm heterosexual but I was never interested in watching men or looking at men's bodies, it was curiosity for women, for women's anatomy, women's pleasure. I had to learn that I could touch myself because it wasn't something that I had done before.' Reflecting on it now, as a woman in her mid-twenties, she said there'd been an impact in terms of how she felt about her body too. But it was insidious, not something explicit. She didn't realize at the time how much it had soaked into the way she felt. 'I've never really thought about this,' she said, 'but I would clock physical differences. The ways that I was not "perfect" like them in terms of how women are expected to look. So, tiny flat tummy or huge boobs. Sizeable bum or no body hair whatsoever. That's what I would pick up on, I guess. How traditionally perfect the women on screen looked and how I was not.'

After being introduced by that boyfriend to porn, Marie had used it every now and then herself. They broke up three years ago and she'd continued doing it off and on, more ambivalent than committed, never finding anything she really liked. But then, eighteen months before we spoke, Marie was raped by a man she had met at a club and it had completely changed how she felt. 'I don't watch anything any more,' she said. 'I just don't want to engage with it. The rape was the start of me learning more about feminism, and the more I read, the less I liked porn.' She told me she started coming across articles talking about exploitation and violence against women in the industry, and this made her feel like she didn't want to support it. She also talked about something like the Clit List, though she couldn't remember the name. It still didn't feel like something she wanted; the whole idea of porn now just turned her off. 'I've never felt the desire to look for that ethical stuff, to go and click on any links and watch any of it,' she said. 'I don't know if that will come back one day, but for now, I don't want much to do with any of it. That's a large part to do with what happened to me.'

Though Marie and Nell both felt that they couldn't risk seeing anything that looked like violence after the violence done to them, they were aware that some women felt differently. It was part of what Harper had talked about, and an idea that has been called 'curative kink'. Nell spoke to me about it explicitly. 'One thing that I find really interesting in the survivor of sexual assault community, or whatever you call it, is that whole thing of people being interested in exploring the boundaries of consent,' she said. 'They explore it in porn, in their sexual relationships, whereas I would find that anxiety-inducing. I think I find it complicated, the possibility that porn could be a tool. Is it really going to be the thing that'll get me over the fact I was violently raped? I'm just not sure I believe that.'

There are exploratory studies that look into this, where people with experiences of abuse prior to adulthood talk about using BDSM to help work through what has been done to them. Here researchers suggest that some people can use some of the safety and sexual practices associated with bondage, domination and sado-masochism to do things like help reframe traumatic experiences, set boundaries and have these respected, and transcend painful memories. Essentially, that specific aspects of BDSM may help some people work through sexual abuse. Another exploratory study found that female survivors of family psychological violence and sexual violence were significantly more likely to watch porn, especially what they thought of as violent porn, than women without this kind of history.[9] Interestingly, no such association was found among the men they studied with experiences of violence; a finding which says something important perhaps about the different drivers for our porn use. The authors mentioned a range of reasons that might help explain this, such as seeking out porn to help understand or normalize what happened, or reliving the violence in order to control it. Joy thought there could be another reason, and it was an idea that she'd come to without judgement attached through reflecting on her own experiences with an abusive man.

'I've had to contend with the fact that my sexual script was developed within situations of sexual violence,' she told me. 'I've had to own the fact that some parts of my sexuality are rooted in that and it has created a connection between power and arousal. I wouldn't say that I'm the only person who has that, but admitting it to myself is difficult because it's not easy to change sexual scripts. You can't really go back and do a lot about that, and we don't really get the space to discuss it.' There's a risk that exploring something like this can reduce sexual desire to an effect of sexual violence. Turning our agency into the consequence of somebody else's; moving from what we want to do, back to a focus on what's done to us. That risk is why these conversations just aren't being had. And we're left – like Joy – to put the pieces together in silence by ourselves.

The past decade has seen what can only be described as a global reckoning on sexual violence. From the revelations of sexual harassment in #MeToo to the experiences of girls and young women at school shared online through sites like Everyone's Invited, it feels like the threat and reality of sexual violence in women's lives is finally being recognized. What does that mean for porn? For a long time, talking about violence in porn has been shut down as being sex negative. It's been argued as being simplistic, as some kind

of moral crusade that judges the choices of performers and users. All that has meant is that some
of us have questions that we can't ask. And a conflict that sits underneath our use that we don't know
how to talk about. There's not one way that porn
is implicated in violence and there's not one way
that we're affected. But we need to acknowledge
that there is a relationship there, because some of
us have lived it.

FUTURE

The future of porn

AT THE START OF THIS book, I talked about the growth of the porn industry over the past few decades and how a lot of this has been fuelled by changes in technology. Porn 2.0 was all about user-participation, ease of access and an endless stream of content. These days we're too used to that; we need something more. Enter Porn 3.0. Now, you're no longer watching porn, you're *in* the porn. This is the metaverse. It's hard for me to write anything here that'll stand the test of time. I'm not the most tech-savvy of people, I've never really got into science fiction, and you need a good basis in both to be able to predict where we're headed. But I do know enough to see that we're on the cusp of the next major change in how we understand our world. It's more a concept than a reality at the moment, but then so was the internet not that long ago.

You've no doubt heard the term 'metaverse' by now. It comes from a nineties science-fiction novel by the American author Neal Stephenson called *Snow Crash*, a book which also popularized the term 'avatar' to mean the online representation of yourself. Essentially, the metaverse refers to a 3D version of the internet which, unlike our current experiences of virtual reality (VR) environments, is interconnected not just with an isolated ecosystem but an entire universe. It's like a massive, multiplayer, multidimensional world which incorporates the user interaction of Internet 2.0 but with the added component of complete immersion. Instead of the online world being held at a distance from the world that we are in and contained by the screen we're in front of, the metaverse merges the two together using augmented reality (AR) headsets to put us inside the action. You could go to a concert, the beach, buy and try on clothes, get a haircut, all through an avatar – your avatar – *you*. You'll be able to move through different virtual worlds created by different companies, as seamlessly as we walk from the warmth of our homes to outside our front door. It's like a doppelgänger universe, without the constraints of our physical world. It's not hard to see the appeal.

The coronavirus pandemic did some of the work needed here to merge our on- and offline worlds. Even a few years ago, the idea of holding a 'hybrid' meeting was unthinkable, let alone a virtual funeral. The technology isn't quite where it needs to be, there are still bad connections and legacy hands, but Covid pushed us to connect online in ways we'd never before thought possible. It's only a matter of time until the tech catches up, particularly when everyone is racing to be the first to get there.

In 2021, Facebook founder and CEO, Mark Zuckerberg, announced that he was changing the company's name to Meta Platforms Inc., or Meta for short. While the platforms the company currently owns remain the same – Facebook, Instagram and WhatsApp, for example – they are all now held under the parent company, Meta. The change was a signal about how much the then Facebook wanted to lead on the metaverse, as well as how confident Zuckerberg was that this is the future of the internet. It's been claimed Meta has invested at least $10 billion in the metaverse already and, given how right Zuckerberg was about social media, I'm going to take his word for it that he's onto something. It's not just Meta that is putting so many of its eggs in the metaverse's virtual basket. The gaming industry, for example, stands to win big time if the metaverse goes mainstream. Epic Games is the owner of Fortnite, one of the popular video game-based 'metaverses' that existed before the term was even popularized. In 2022, *Forbes* reported Epic was investing heavily in the metaverse infrastructure developer Hadean, in the hope of scaling everything up to create an entire virtual ecosystem.[1] Other Big Tech companies are in on the act too – Apple, Google, Microsoft and Sony have all made substantial investments (with Apple set to launch its first 'mixed reality' headset) – and Nike and Disney have jumped in as well, already working out how to capitalize on the new marketplace the metaverse will give them. It looks like all the major players think this is the next big thing. They're so certain that it's something they've put their money where their mouth is, and the porn industry is no exception.

*

Though virtual sex is currently excluded from the activities Meta is building into its vision of the metaverse, word is that the porn industry is investing heavily in products to help augment users' online sexual experiences. Global economic forecasts have predicted the market for VR porn to be worth over $1 billion by 2025. From the fun-to-say teledildonics – essentially Bluetooth-enabled sex toys – which can be used to create immersive webcam shows where users control the vibrations of the webcammer's sex toy, to things like haptic gloves which give users an experience of realistic touch through advanced tactile feedback, there's huge scope for immersive porn once the technology catches up. Speaking to the *Sun* newspaper in 2022, a spokesperson for DreamCam – a company which advertises itself as 'the one and only VR webcam platform' for the adult entertainment industry – claimed that porn in the metaverse will feel better than real sex, and estimated that the 'sextech' needed to do it may hit the market in just a year or two.[2] Knowing what we do about how the online porn industry makes most of its money these days, this kind of focus and investment in technology development makes sense. The surveillance capitalism model under-pinning companies such as Aylo can be taken to a whole new level in the metaverse. Augmented reality headsets are not only giving you information about the virtual world you're in, they're sending – you guessed it – data about you onto the company that owns them. A lot of data. VR headsets can track and transmit bodily information like eye movements, pupil dilation, facial expressions and body temperature. This means that they can use bodily cues that we can't control to identify exactly what it is that gets us going and then auction this information off to advertisers to get us to buy what they're selling.

It's also not the first time the porn industry has played a major role in pushing technology further, something that Pornhub's then vice president, Corey Price, noted in 2018 when announcing Pornhub's move to accepting crypto-currency. In a press release on the change, Price is quoted as saying that 'History has proven that the adult entertainment industry plays a critical role in adoption for innovative technology. We saw that with VHS, Beta Max, credit card payment icons and, most recently, VR goggles.'[3] Though there's been some speculation as to whether a Pornhub employee called 'Corey

Price' actually exists – an investigation by *Business Insider* comes up blank for any backstory to Price prior to representing Pornhub from 2011 – this acknowledgement of porn's role in tech is fairly well recognized. From the VCR to the internet itself, it's been said that the porn industry has not only helped finance technological developments, it's also played a key role in user take-up, particularly in the early days of both when the equipment was expensive and the quality was sketchy at the best of times. All of which means that while Meta might not want sex in the metaverse, it might be exactly what ends up getting us all there to take a look around. It's been claimed, for example, that already 'porn' is the number one search term associated with virtual reality (more than VR games or VR apps) and that more than two thirds of VR headset users in the UK and US have used their devices to watch porn.[4] The figures for the latter claim are, unsurprisingly, higher for men than for women. But some women are getting in on it too, and Katherine was one of them.

Katherine was almost thirty when we spoke, and the weekend before our conversation, she'd had her first go at virtual reality porn. She'd been

using porn fairly regularly since she first got a
family computer back in her late teens. Like a lot
of women, she started out looking at lesbian porn
on Pornhub, and told me she used the rest of
what she saw to learn what she was supposed to
do in sex. 'I saw porn before I had sex myself,' she
said. 'And for a long time after, when I became
sexually active, I would fake orgasms because I
thought that my role was to convey my pleasure,
so that the guy could feel good.' She told me she
did that for many years until she learned she had
a right to say what she liked and what she didn't.
But once she discovered that, she'd been more
comfortable exploring herself sexually, and part
of that was testing out virtual worlds and porn.
'We got given this headset for Christmas and
I hadn't really looked at it but I'd heard about
VR porn and wanted to know what it was like,'
she said. 'Then my husband went away last weekend and I would normally have watched porn
anyway, so I decided I'd give the headset a try.'
While VR porn currently exists, and there are a
number of sites where you can download or
stream content, headsets like the one Katherine
had can be expensive, and though you can use a
smartphone it's far from recommended. It means
that the technology is still out of most people's

hands, and even when it's in them the experience isn't exactly immersive.

For Katherine, it felt very different from porn. It wasn't just about being more interactive; even without her other senses involved it felt like she had an actual presence in it. 'It's a really different experience,' she told me. 'It heightens what you get visually but you don't get anything tactile. It's still enough to feel a lot more like you're there. The other person in it just feels more in your face.' She said that it felt as if she was an active participant rather than passively watching, and it's here that VR porn could perhaps be useful for women – to give us an experience of leading the action and challenge the scripts we inherit about sex. Except, of course, it's not made for us. 'Obviously, it's quite new,' Katherine told me. 'So you can almost see what people think it's relevant to develop. It tries to put the user as if it's their point of view so who they choose to put in that position is interesting, and also who they put them with.' She said she tried out a couple of different scenarios, one where she had the position of a man with a woman, and another with a woman from a woman's point of view. But she said that she noticed there wasn't a heterosexual one from a woman's perspective, something that says probably all it needs to about who the virtual world is currently designed by and for. In the end, Katherine said it was pleasurable but it did get her thinking. 'It's such a completely different experience than just watching porn,' she told me. 'There probably are implications of it for society but I haven't quite figured out what they are yet.' Considering what happens for women in VR worlds more broadly, I get the sense that, whatever they are, these implications might not be all that good for women.

Accounts of sexual harassment, sexual assault, rape and child sexual abuse are mounting across users' experiences of the worlds that will create the metaverse, as are experiences of homophobic and racist violence. It looks as though this brave new world is bringing with it some of the same old problems as our current one. A small pilot study completed in 2017 found that female users of VR technology experienced forms of sexual harassment in VR worlds such as unwanted sexual attention and a lack of respect for personal and physical boundaries.[5] In 2022, a female researcher for the non-profit organization SumOfUs, a charity that campaigns to hold corporations accountable on issues such as climate change, discrimination

and human rights, encountered this first hand.[6]
Within an hour of entering Meta's VR platform,
Horizon Worlds, the woman – through her
avatar – was led into a private room at a party
where she was raped by a user who kept telling
her to turn around so he could do it from behind.
Users outside the window could see and another
user inside the room watched and passed around
a vodka bottle. She had been encouraged by
another user to remove her personal boundaries
settings and she noted that it meant that when
another user touched you, the hand controllers
vibrated – something that makes for a jarring
experience in the real world when being assaulted
in the virtual one. The researcher is quoted in the
charity's report on the platform as saying that the
rape 'happened so fast I kind of disassociated.
One part of my brain was like, wtf is happening,
the other part was like, this isn't a real body, and
another part was like, this is important research.'
She described the entire experience as disorient-
ing and confusing. And it's not the first time this
kind of thing has happened. Back in 2018, a
seven-year-old girl from America reported her
avatar being raped by two male avatars when the
children-focused VR gaming platform Roblox was
hacked.[7] Sitting beside her mother playing the

game, the girl suddenly turned to her distressed. Her mum was able to shield her from seeing what was happening, as two male avatars raped her avatar on a school playground, and a female observer came over and jumped on the girl's body, before all three ran off. Though Roblox responded quickly, recent reports from the BBC suggest the platform is now being regularly used to sexually groom children, and YouTube is still filled with videos about how to 'rape hack' Roblox so you can sexually assault its userbase, made up mostly of children under the age of thirteen.[8] Both of these virtual assaults took place without the full sensory immersion planned for the metaverse through haptics and bodily sensors. If they did, it would have been much harder to separate the real physical self from what was happening to its virtual representation. After all, that's the point.

Less than a year before the virtual rape experienced by the SumOfUs researcher, London-based mother of three and researcher on 'extended reality' (the catch-all name for things like AR or VR) Nina Jane Patel spoke out about experiencing sexual harassment and assault across the then Facebook's VR venues.[9] Patel said that an avatar she had created to resemble herself was assaulted within a minute of joining Horizon Venues – now part of Horizon Worlds – by three to four male avatars. The men surrounded her, groped her, subjected her to a stream of sexual innuendo, took screenshots of the attack, and yelled, 'Don't pretend you didn't love it!' as she tried to get away. Patel has experienced anxiety ever since, and looked into the reasons why – even though the assault didn't happen to her physical self – it's had such an impact on her in the real world. It turns out it's pretty simple. Virtual reality has been designed to be completely immersive; the whole point of it is to trick the mind and body into feeling like virtual experiences are real. We might, like that researcher, be able to know on the one hand that what we're seeing isn't a real body, but on the other everything around us is designed to make us feel like it is.

Though this immersive aspect is an important consideration, it is also true that violence against women and girls does not need to be physical to cause harm. We know this already about other forms of online and sexual harassment, which can leave us feeling violated while our body remains untouched. But other than complain to the platform or come offline, there's little anyone is able to do about it. If the metaverse removes the constraints of the physical world, meaning we can virtually teleport to work, the shops, back home, it will also remove other limitations we have in real life, and legislation is one of them. Just as governments worldwide have struggled with a lack of jurisdiction over the internet, their laws will also have no authority in a world that doesn't really exist, no matter how real it feels to us. And here's where we get to the crux of what porn in the metaverse might mean for women.

If what's been happening already is anything to go by, the live VR webcamming of platforms such as DreamCam, not to mention the multi-player virtual sex worlds that many users are pinning their hopes on, could be extremely dangerous for women. While it might never reach Zuckerberg's vision of interconnected, immersive virtual worlds, it seems almost inevitable given the investment that some kind of change is coming in that borderline between what's online and off. The same elements that are being lauded as the benefits of virtual porn – the fact users can try out acts they might not want to do in person, or can feel as though they're actually touching and being touched by others even though they're in their bedroom alone – could be used to create new forms of violence, harassment and intimidation that will restrict women in the virtual world in much the same way as we're restricted in this one. The things many women do in our day-to-day life to feel safe in public spaces – our safety work – already translates to the ways we limit ourselves online: choosing particular settings and only using certain platforms, limiting what we say or what's in our profile to reduce the risk of harassment. But it's not only in the metaverse itself that there's the potential for fallout. We've heard stories from women in their twenties about how much they learned from porn – Bonita and River talking about how porn functioned as a form of instruction, a blueprint for what to expect will be expected of them. Women in their thirties and forties, like Imogen and Annemarie, have talked about the practices of men, saying younger clients' requests had changed shape over the past ten years as porn has become what it is today. What will this mean when porn becomes embodied and we take in what it teaches us through all of our senses? What might this amplify? What might it allow? And what could be the impact of these changes for the girls coming up behind us?

The next generation

Each year, the social research company NatCen publishes the British Social Attitudes Survey. It's a fairly reliable overview of where we're at as a society on topical issues such as immigration and the consequences of Brexit. In 2017, the survey explored moral issues, and pornography use was one of them.[10] The survey asked whether adults should be able to watch whatever porn they wanted, as well as whether it was wrong to do this in their own homes. But for young people's use it only asked about teenage boys, as if no one else is watching. It's an omission that needs addressing because, just two years later, a study from the British Board of Film Classification found that adults are particularly out of step with what we know about young people and porn.[11] Drawing from a survey of over 2,000 young people and their parents, as well as in-depth interviews with both groups, they found that more than half (51 per cent) of 11–13-year-olds had seen porn at some point, rising to a third (66 per cent) of 14–15-year-olds. Children described feeling 'grossed out' and 'confused', particularly those who had seen porn when they were under ten. But one of the most concerning parts of all was that their parents,

overwhelmingly, had no idea, and this was particularly the case when it came to girls. A third of
parents thought their sons would have seen porn,
whereas over two thirds of the boys actually had.
Only 17 per cent (less than a fifth) thought the
same thing of their daughters, despite the fact that
over half of the girls had seen it. That's not just a
different ballpark, it's an entirely different game.
It's that familiar denial of female sexuality and the
silence around our desire. We're not thinking
about girls as actively seeking out porn and it
means we're not talking to them about what they
might find.

Zara worked for a sexual health charity and told
me she felt quite conflicted by porn. She didn't
think it was necessarily a good or bad thing; more
that it was like fast food – an easy fix that ultimately could be better. 'I feel like a lot of young
women don't have great sex, which I find quite
sad,' she said. 'And I don't think of porn as a force
for bad or for good. It has the potential to be
decent but the vast majority isn't.' Approaching
her late twenties now, Zara said she came to porn
relatively late. And like the research showing
some positives from teenagers' use, she told me
she'd seen some benefits of using it, both for

herself and society more broadly. 'I think sometimes it can be quite nice to just be focusing on
yourself. You're giving yourself pleasure and
nobody else has to be involved,' she told me. 'And
porn's played a role in us seeing sex as important,
we're seeing more diversity in sex too. So, things
that twenty, thirty years ago, you might have been
shunned for liking, you can talk about them now
and everyone would be like, "Oh, how interesting, tell me more."'

Though Zara thought porn could be useful,
she also said that she was concerned. It wasn't
based on moral conservatism or panic – that
much-derided call of 'won't somebody think of
the children'. It was based on her own experiences
and wanting it to be easier for the girls coming
behind her. 'I don't want to be overdramatic and
I don't want to overstate the effects that pornography might have, but I do think that now it's so
accessible and people see so much of it before
they've even had sex,' she said. 'I'm not saying
that it's terrible and nobody's ever going to have
good sex again, but I do think that it's going to
mean young people learn certain things and it's
going to take them time to unlearn them.' For
Zara this wasn't a new challenge for young
women; it was something we've all dealt with

before. All those messages we get about our bodies and our desire – pornography doesn't create them, but the vast majority of it doesn't challenge them either. 'There were certain things I had to unlearn as well,' she told me. 'There was so much crap that filled my head through teen magazines or films when I was younger and then I hit a certain age and started talking to other people. And I think this is another thing now. That once young people grow into adults and start having relationships and more sex, they're going to have to learn to unlearn porn if they want to have their own authentic experiences.'

When I was a teenager, my main source for information about sex and the female body was the advice columns in teen magazines. Though they've all but died out now, magazines pitched at the 13–17-year-old girl market were big business in the eighties, nineties and early 2000s. There were the adolescent versions of established names, like *Teen Vogue* and *Teen People*, and then those which set out to establish their own unique brand like the UK's *More* with its 'position of the fortnight' and *Just Seventeen*, a magazine whose problem pages tend to evoke fond memories from most of the women I've spoken to. In

Australia, where I grew up, the market was dominated by a magazine called *Dolly* that contained a coveted sealed section where readers would have their questions about health, sexuality and female anatomy answered by an anonymous female doctor. Pre-internet, these magazines felt like the only place you could get detailed information about sex and our bodies, and for that I am forever indebted to them. But it's disturbing revisiting *Dolly*'s cover stories as a woman in my forties. Thirteen-year-old girls advised on 'which exercise programme is best for you', 'fun ways to lose fat fast', 'After school pig outs, how to stop and eat healthy'. Articles on swimming costumes that 'make you look slim', all written by adults for an adolescent market.

Looking back on them now, I think most of us can see that while there were some benefits, what we learned wasn't great. I learned to compare myself to other women, for example, to focus too much on what I looked like and too little on what I thought. I took some useful tips about blowjobs and masturbation, but also the sense that the measure of women was how desired they were by men. It's taken me years – like Zara – to undo this, and I'm sure that some of it is still lurking in the back of my mind. That's part of what's being said here when women say they're concerned. When you ask women what they think about porn, those who watch it and those who don't, those who love it and those who've not seen it, across our different experiences one thing stands out: we're worried about the age kids can see the same porn that we can. This isn't about hysteria or misguided attempts to protect the innocence of youth. It's largely based on knowing how much girls take on about who and how we should be, and how hard that is to shake. It also isn't just about women of my generation, scared of the technological advances that have meant the world looks very different for our children. Younger women in their late teens and early twenties said something similar. And Helena was one of them.

Helena was twenty-two and grew up with the internet. She thought it was something that marked a line in the sand in relation to young people's experiences of porn. 'I think it makes a massive difference, whether or not you had the internet. It means that, even among people who are of a similar age, they can have entirely different experiences around pornography, just because of how quickly the internet has grown,' she told me. 'I think it's even different now from when I grew up, not just because we access the internet

more from a young age, but because it can be
quite easily private. More people have the internet on their phone so you would never need to be
concerned about anyone knowing what you had
looked at or having any real restriction on it. You
can watch it completely privately and no one
would really know.'

Despite growing up with a lot of this access,
Helena had never actually used porn. She said
she'd heard jokes being made about it at school at
fifteen, so she looked it up once just out of curiosity,
didn't like what she saw, and never bothered again.
But though Helena didn't use it, she was surrounded by people her age and younger who did,
and she was worried about what they were learning from it, something she felt was connected to
the silence about sex more broadly. 'I think it is
not just to do with sex education in schools, but
also to do with how a lot of subjects around sexuality are still very taboo,' she said. 'A lot of parents
don't feel comfortable talking to their children
about sex and a lot of young people won't feel
comfortable talking to their friends about it. So, it
means that people get their ideas from porn
because there's nowhere else to go to.' She was
worried about what they were learning from
porn, and thought the representations of women

and race were horrific. She also felt that its impact went further than affecting just those who use it; that its messages spread out and change not just what young people do but how they think as well. 'People in my generation have got a lot of their ideas about sex from porn and I think it is really important to talk about,' she said. 'I've seen it shape attitudes in a really big way, even if you don't watch it yourself.'

Frances was the same age as Helena; she'd told me the split between slut and whore dominated attitudes at her school. She also had a similar position to Helena on porn, but she felt that some of the problem here was about how adults respond to the sexual expression of girls. She told me she first saw porn online at eight years old after googling sex with a friend. 'I have a strange memory of me and this other girl,' she said. 'We were in primary school together in Year Four. We were at one of our houses, and she was like, "Look, I google-imaged sex," and showed me what she found.' Frances remembers going home after that and looking it up for herself. She said she was horrified by what she saw but there was also a curious fascination. She didn't seek porn out by herself after that, but it wasn't only because of that experience. She said it was more about the combination of jealousy and judgement that she was taught to feel about female desire. It was an attitude that she felt was replicated in most porn through the way it positioned women as objects, primarily for the male gaze. But it was also a sense of women and sex that she'd learned from the adults around her, even ones who probably felt like they were doing the right thing.

'There was a huge scandal in my school when a naked picture of a girl circulated online and the whole school went nuts,' she told me. 'It was a naked picture that she had taken – she was sixteen – I think it was to send to her boyfriend. It was very graphic, legs spread, but it was actually quite tasteful, like black and white. Her boyfriend had circulated it everywhere and people were then just sending it around. Everyone in my school saw it because it was just popping up on people's newsfeeds. A girl in Year Eight copied this older girl, and then it got really serious.' She told me the school brought the police in, and they had a big assembly that everyone had to attend. The girl who'd taken the images of herself in the first place was there and what happened to her, Frances said, was etched in her mind. 'Our head-mistress was giving a speech about how we have to respect ourselves and the girl was sitting there laughing. I imagine in self-defence, because what else could she do? The headmistress, in front of the whole school – there was about eight hundred of us in this massive hall – saw what she was doing and got her to stand up and said, "I am horrified that you would laugh, when it is your actions which have brought this school into disrepute." She made her leave the hall in front of everyone.' Frances said she didn't see the girl again after that; she thought she'd been expelled. And when she looks back on it now, she feels dreadful about how the girl was treated. 'At the time, we all thought that this was her fault. We all had the same opinion that she had done something ridiculous,' she said. 'I look back and I feel filled with horror about that whole scenario because she did nothing wrong.' Frances's story shows how careful we need to be in addressing the next generation. Because we're bringing to them what we've learned ourselves about who is allowed to be sexual, and how.

As I write this, government attempts to limit children and young people's access to porn – both in the UK and worldwide – have been complicated, to say the least. It seems that globally policy-makers are grappling with how to respond appropriately to the fact that porn companies are profiting off children accessing their content, regularly and illegally. I'm not talking about countries that have sought to ban pornography outright, though there are a number of those, including China, Iran, Thailand and Turkey. This is about countries trying to regulate pornography online in the ways they do offline, ensuring their laws can be applied, including limiting access for those under the age of eighteen. South Africa, Australia, Germany, Italy and Ireland are among the many who've been looking for an answer. And they'll all be looking to France over the next few years as it's set to be the first country to actually bring in controls. France is introducing a digital certificate – what's been called a 'porn passport' by some in the press – requiring anyone watching pornography online to prove they are over eighteen. Details of the plans were announced in 2023 and will work through users installing a government app on their phones; working, in the words of France's digital minister, 'like the verification requested by your bank when you make an online purchase'.[12] In some ways this is made easier in France because it already requires everyone to possess some form of valid government-issued identity documentation. This is not the case in the UK, which is part of the reason we've been struggling with age verification on and off for a decade.

In 2013, the then UK Prime Minister David Cameron made an impassioned pledge that his government would be making sure that the same rules apply online as they do offline; or as he said, 'Put simply: what you can't get in a shop, you shouldn't be able to get online.'[13] Four years later the UK became the first country to have a legal mandate on the provision of age verification for pornographic websites, only to have this dropped in 2019 due to privacy and technical issues, and picked up again in 2021 with the Online Safety Bill. In October 2023 the Bill gained Royal Assent, becoming the Online Safety Act and bringing age verification back for the UK. The Act places a duty of care on many companies that operate online to protect their users from harm. This includes legal requirements for platforms that come within its scope and publish pornography to have robust processes in place to check that a user is not underage. However, unlike in France, while the government regulator Ofcom will check these processes, what they actually are is left up to the sites themselves and therein lies the problem. Because our old friend Aylo, back when they were MindGeek, can spot a business – and data – opportunity from a mile away.

In 2015, in the midst of the first attempts at age verification in the UK, the then MindGeek set up an independent company called AgeID. The company intended to provide a 'simple and secure solution' for all other porn sites needing to validate the age of users.[14] This meant that before the age verification proposals were dropped in 2019, MindGeek stood to make millions from the implementation of the UK's legislation; originally intended to regulate its industry, it was set to further embed its monopoly. But it's not just because age verification stood to make MindGeek millions that the issue is much more complicated than Cameron's initial speech made it seem. There are also ongoing concerns about data security: essentially that requiring porn users to somehow log in will make it easier for the sites to collect – and for someone to possibly leak – information on an individual's viewing habits. It's part of why age verification has been roundly rejected by the American courts for decades, citing it as in contravention of the First Amendment of the US constitution – the one that protects freedom of expression. And it's also why so many countries will be looking to France, which claims its system of digital certification – which isn't left up to the sites to decide themselves – will protect personal data from being accessed by third parties, including porn companies and their advertisers. On top of all this, there's also the issue of what happens to smaller producers; systems for age verification are costly and many might struggle to bring them in. MindGeek originally offered its AgeID solution to independent porn producers for free, though since the 2023 rebrand whether this offer still stands is unclear. If it does, what it will mean for the ability of independent producers' to question Aylo's business practices is an unanswered question. It seems like the whole area is a bomb that keeps ticking while we're frantically trying to work out which wire to cut. There are clear consequences for not acting, but there might be unintended ones if we do.

As someone who made porn herself, not to sell but to share online, the push for age verification was something that impacted Molly directly. Molly was a white woman in her mid-forties with two almost fully grown children. It was only really in the past decade that she felt she'd come into herself sexually, and got to the point where she now posted publicly about her sex life, BDSM and the dominant/submissive relationship she had with her husband. Before that she was married to another man, had two young kids and was sexually bored. She had thought that was her lot, until she went online in her mid-thirties. Suddenly the world opened up. 'I'd spent many years feeling like there was something missing,' she told me. 'I was doing this thing and being this thing but it was like making a puzzle all the time and every time I put it together there were a couple of pieces missing. Then I discovered more about the internet. I found places online where I could read erotic fiction and watch porn. I discovered my chat rooms and people who were talking openly about sex and I think that awakened me to the fact that something really radical had to change in my life. Something was very wrong.' She separated from her husband, started dating, and has never really looked back. She went from feeling divorced from her sexuality to being in control of it, and reflecting on that shift she thought pornography had played a big role. 'I think porn is like a poke in the eye to what society tells us about sex,' she said. 'Like, no, there is fucking and there is fucking for pleasure and here are people doing it, and it's fucking hot. It helped set me on a road to realizing what I needed and wanted as a basic part of my life.'

Partly to map this journey for herself as well as give back to the online communities that helped her, Molly had set up an online blog where she posted intimate photos of herself, wrote stories and shared fantasies, as well as saving images that represented what got her off. For her, it begun as a personal project but she'd developed quite a following. It meant that even though she was making no money from it, she'd still have to implement whatever the government decided for porn sites, which would cost and could ultimately stop her posting. 'I think the government in the UK is making it increasingly harder for people producing ethical, feminist or female-gaze porn. They don't have the financial resources to implement age verification,' she told me. 'So, the big boys of porn are going to get bigger, stronger, they are going to dominate the porn market even more than they have, and they're going to push those other smaller companies backwards and possibly out of business completely.' But the answer wasn't to just do nothing; instead, Molly thought we needed to give kids knowledge – for the government to take the millions it was spending on legislating and put it into age-appropriate sex education from five years old through to university. She also saw a role for women, to talk to the next generation in order to change the narrative we inherited on female sexuality – the one that for years had held her back. 'One of the things that I've taught my kids is that the main purpose of sex for humans is pleasure. Just that message still continues to be missing, particularly for girls,' she said. 'The whole thing about you can have a completely fantastic and legitimate sexual experience on your own is missing for women and girls. That this isn't meant to be just sex and your body. It's meant to be about pleasure.' Whatever happens with government policy, the need for this message remains. It's something we probably need to hear more ourselves if we're ever going to get to somewhere different.

The future for us

At seventy, Polly was one of the oldest women I spoke to. She gave me a real sense of how things have changed over time for women, porn and pleasure, and the idea of sexual liberation. Watching what's been happening in the world recently, she had a sense we were falling backwards. As if we'd forgotten the lessons of the past and were sleepwalking into something that's not good for any of us. 'My dad was a Jewish refugee,' she told me. 'He came from Europe in 1939, fleeing from the Nazis. But I think the violence, the cruelty, Trump, Brexit, you name it, it's all about a lust for power. It's like we've turned the clock back to the thirties, with Stalin and Hitler and Mussolini and Franco. There are good things, but it's very precarious. It's always been precarious, I guess.' Polly talked to me about coming of age as a young white woman in London in the swinging sixties. She spoke about London's artworld, and how her kids were jealous of her adolescence in what felt like the centre of the world. 'It was fantastic, growing up in the sixties. I mean, nothing was better than the sixties,' she said. 'I was fifteen/ sixteen when the Beatles started, fifteen/sixteen with the Rolling Stones. Everything was just – the world was exploding. We thought everything was going to be hippy and free and wonderful.' It was a world where she said porn didn't really have a place – something that shows how much can change in just a generation. 'Nobody was watching porn in the sixties, and nobody talked about porn,' she told me. 'I had one friend who was an artist and had a famous porn collection because it was part of his art shtick, and, honestly, he probably couldn't get sex any other way. He was very little and very "man/woman/frog or goat" is what my friend said about him, but he was the only person I knew. Porn was for dirty old men, like people's fathers, with their *Playboys*. We didn't need it. We had sex.'

The picture of porn and its users that Polly painted seemed a world apart from what we have today, but when she laid it out over the course of her lifetime it didn't seem that long ago. I asked her what she thought had happened that changed the trajectory she felt we were on. And she came back with a one-word answer that made me think of Aylo and the money the company is making from the conflict women are having. 'Capitalism,' she said. 'What happened was we got Thatcher and the eighties. The whole thing of money came in. People wanted to be in business suits and high heels, and all that. It's horrendous, actually, what has happened to women since the sixties.' For Polly, the seventies contained possibilities that were intercepted by the search for profit. It was this that diverted the sexual revolution, taking women in a different direction from where she thought we were headed. 'Liberation is finding someone you like that just likes you back,' she said. 'It's very liberating to find reciprocity. But capitalism keeps us apart on purpose and pornography plays into that. Obviously, you did filthy, dirty things when you're getting into sex. God, I was doing that in my forties, with a boyfriend I had for seven years. It was very liberating but it wasn't pornography. It was about people, not parts. There's a big difference, isn't there?'

There is an essay written by the Black feminist poet Audre Lorde called 'The Uses of the Erotic: The Erotic as Power' that has been in my mind over the years as I've been talking and thinking about porn. It came from a paper that Lorde gave at a conference on the History of Women in the summer of 1978. For Lorde the erotic is a resource for power, and it's one that has been vilified and devalued within western society. She argues that the erotic has been misnamed by men and misused against women, confused with its opposite, the pornographic. But where pornography emphasizes sensation without feeling, the 'erotic' – from the Greek word *eros* meaning 'love' – is the word for the very depth of feeling itself. 'For the erotic is not a question only of what we can do,' Lorde says, 'it is a question of how acutely and fully we can feel in the doing.'[15] The erotic is about creative power and harmony, the name for that sense of self-connection which bridges our pleasure and our principles. When we feel it we are able to stand in our power, and demand from our world and ourselves that which brings us joy. But the word 'erotic' was noticeably absent from most of the conversations I've had. Though porn has helped different women at different times in different ways, I could count on one hand the number who talked about it as joyous.

Understanding the erotic in the way that Audre Lorde does is a change to how – and where – we've been taught to find it, because it's not about, or not only about, the erotic being something sexual. When we look, Lorde says, eroticism is everywhere: in writing a poem, the way our bodies stretch to music, the joy of building a bookcase. It's about being present in our lives and in ourselves, and seeing each other as whole people. It's that deep connection to our bodies that is rarely encouraged for women; about feeling our bodies as something we are, not something we have to control and compare. I was reminded of this in something Isobel told me about a talk she went to for work; this sense that even with sex we can forget that – as Molly said – it's meant to be about pleasure.

As a GP, not only had Isobel noticed a change in women's grooming practices, she also spent a lot of time going to various information events, taking notes for her practice, hoping one day it'd come in handy. They were normally quite dry sessions, a PowerPoint, then a bit of a chat, but on one occasion it was different and changed how she thought about sex for herself. 'There was a really good talk I went to when I attended a Family Planning and Reproductive Healthcare update,' she told me. 'One bit of it was about somebody who was a sex and relationship counsellor and was mainly talking about the menopause, but then she started talking about some quotes by somebody called Leonore Tiefer. It said something like, "Sex is not a natural act like breathing. It's like dancing. Some people are good at it and some people are not, but most people can learn how to make it better." The metaphor was something like the difference between dancing and digestion. With digestion, everybody does it much the same way and sometimes something goes wrong with it and you can try and put it right. Whereas with dancing, there are lots of different styles; have a go and it doesn't matter what you look like. Some people might be ballerinas and some might be doing dad dancing, but as long as you are enjoying it, it doesn't really matter.'

Leonore Tiefer is an American clinical psychologist and long-time feminist activist who has written extensively on sex and women, and this metaphor captures one of her most widely recognized ideas – that sex isn't natural in the way we often think it is. It's full of cultural meanings about how we do it and why. Sex is like dancing: there's no one right or wrong way. The point is to dance for the joy and the freedom it brings; to dance for yourself, when and how you want to. This is exactly what Lorde meant when she talked about the power of the erotic. She believed that if we truly saw the erotic as being that depth of feeling then we would stop settling for what is convenient, what is conventionally expected, shoddy or safe. We would stop living outside ourselves, following external directives about the shape our life should take, including the shape of our sexual expression. When we recognize and seize our own eroticism – connect fully with the depth of feeling it is possible for us to have –

Lorde says we will pursue genuine change in our world rather than settle for the same weary drama. It's that change we need for our future. And after all the conversations I've had I have to say I'm not sure porn gets us closer to it.

Like Polly, Jay was also seventy when we spoke, but she came with a different background and it brought a very different experience. Though they were both white, Jay was a working-class lesbian who was involved with a range of radical feminist groups at the time that Polly was at the heart of London's art scene. Considering her decades of involvement in the women's movement, and years of thinking through the questions I was grappling with, I thought she'd have some insight into where we've been and where we're heading. And she did, but not in the way I expected.

'It's hard to know what sexual freedom even means for women,' she told me. 'But maybe I'm just cynical in my old age. I think empowerment and control for women changes, between cultures, through history. But when I think about how things shift and turn, it is only the edges of it that change.' Talking to Jay gave me a sense that the things women had told me about their bodies and desire, about sex and relationships and their experiences of violence, weren't new or unexpected. The edges changed across generations and backgrounds but the struggle with it all remained. Free mainstream porn clearly didn't start the fire, and the questions and debates that we're having now are the same that we've been having for decades. There might be an intensity – an urgency – now, but the basic outline of the issue is unchanged. 'We were trying to work porn out back then,' Jay said about the eighties and nineties. 'Perhaps like you are now. We wanted to know what use it was and how we should deal with it. But there never seemed to be any space for compromise on views, or whatever it is called these days, between the different positions. In the early days a lot of people were arguing about where you draw the line. I think those arguments are long; I suppose people might still have them. I just always thought, yes, you are drawing lines all over women's bodies.'

When I look back on everything women have said, it's this that I keep coming back to, the lines drawn across and between us, the divisions and silences they leave. The debate about women and porn will rage on, I'm sure, but something lies beneath it which is much less disputed. And it's this, more than anything, that I'm left with. It can take the better part of women's lives to feel like the pleasure we give ourselves is legitimate. Years spent denying we masturbate, whole decades passing without knowing what our own bodies look like. And porn is a big part of that journey; brought in by a partner, or used alone, or just out there in that cultural space telling us what sex and sexuality should look like. Porn has and continues to play a role in moving us forward and pulling us back, but largely this has all been unspoken. Hidden from ourselves and from each other. It's time to bring it out into the open.

Whether we want it to be there or not, pornography is threaded through our lives. It's surrounding ourselves and our partners, our co-workers and our teachers, our friends and our children. What that means for women is complex and more than a single story. What the women I've spoken to told me changed what I thought I knew about what we did and why. It's a tangled web of messages about desire and our bodies, about who we're told sex is for and what happens when women ask for it. It's about our relationship to ourselves and to our sexual partners, and the violence so many of us have lived through and are living with today. Ultimately, it's about the future and the conversations we need to have to change it. This is really what I'm left with. After all, if we're going to be the fish who points out the water, first we need to be willing to see it ourselves.

AFTERWORD

THERE HAVE BEEN SOME SIGNIFICANT changes since I started this research. The platform OnlyFans exploded in popularity over Covid, providing a subscription service for users wanting pornographic content, and a platform for creators to engage directly with their customers. The use of generative AI has come on leaps and bounds, to the point where it is being harnessed to create realistic looking pornographic images out of everyday photos, 'deepfakes', which have then been used to harass, intimidate, and humiliate girls as young as eleven.[1] Pornhub has introduced new measures to prohibit users from searching for some kinds of violent content, such as porn depicting rape. And the conversation about the role of recommendation algorithms in driving us towards extreme content has grown louder, including some recognition about how this shapes the porn we watch (though not yet how that might be shaping our desire). Porn really is that shifting target, seemingly always two steps ahead. But it's not the only thing that's changed as I've been doing this work. I feel different now. When I first started writing this book, I thought I had to end with an answer about what porn means for women. That it's not enough to just outline a situation, people want solutions and they want them now. But in fact, at the end, I think that's the last thing that's needed. We don't need more advice and assumptions and judgements, more messages about what we should do. If we want to know about women and porn, we need more space to ask some difficult questions.

Like what comes first, the porn or the desire? Are we seeking out only what we want or are we watching what is brought to us, and how does that feel? How honest are we with our partners about what we've seen and what turns us on? Has porn changed the sex we have? When has that been helpful? When has that harmed? What about the impact on our fantasy life? Has porn wound its way in? Do we want a way out? We might not have been asked these questions before, but that doesn't mean we haven't asked them ourselves. The stories that remain to be told are many. All that we need to do is listen.

ACKNOWLEDGEMENTS

THERE ARE A LOT OF people who have helped make this book what it is but none more so than the women who took part in the research underpinning it. Thank you to every one of the women who contacted me ready to share their stories of porn, and to the one hundred women who spoke to me in the end. I wish I could have you all in a room talking to each other; this book was in part inspired by that desire.

I also want to thank the Leverhulme Trust, who funded the research itself through an early-career fellowship. As a funder they have been incredibly supportive and flexible from the start, and this book would not have been possible without their belief in the project.

To my Child & Women Abuse Studies Unit team at London Metropolitan University: Sukhwant Dhaliwal, Aruna Dudhia, Maria Garner, Liz Kelly, Jo Lovett and Purna Sen. Thank you all for your intelligence, inspiration and insights. Working with you is a dream and I hope it never ends. To Durham University, which housed me during the research for this book, particularly Clare McGlynn and Nicole Westmarland, who are both endless sources of wisdom and humour and kindness.

Publishing this book has been a great experience and I put that down to the women who have made it happen. Thank you to Hayley Steed for her direction early on and to Caroline Hardman for her belief, skill and expertise in getting me over the finish line. Thank you to Tamsin Shelton and Vivien Thompson for their careful edits, and the rest of the team at Penguin Random House – it really does take a village. To Kate Fox, my editor, thank you for believing in this from the get-go. We've been so wonderfully aligned on what this book was about and I've trusted and valued your every instinct. I hope it's turned out how you saw it.

Thank you to Christina and Kelsey, who let me write the bulk of this on their back porch one summer, and Tara, Jason, Jayne and the kids for being the best kind of family. Thanks to Lucybug and my mum, and all my women in Australia and the UK who fill me with love daily. Particular thanks to Claudia for providing such useful feedback early on; you made me one very happy tortilla.

Finally, to Chris and little Spud. What else can I say? You are both the joys of my life and I will love you forever.

NOTES

PREFACE

1 **Searches for porn:** Ogas, O. and Gaddam, S. (2011), *A Billion Wicked Thoughts: What the World's Largest Experiment Reveals about Human Desire*, Dutton/Penguin Books; **Pornhub accessed by 15 million people in the UK:** Ofcom (2021), *Online Nation 2021*, https://www.ofcom.org.uk/__data/assets/pdf_file/0013/220414/online-nation-2021-report.pdf

INTRODUCTION

1 **'Hardcore' showing an erection:** Ciclitira, K. (1998), *What does pornography mean to women?*, PhD thesis, Manchester Metropolitan University
2 **Growth of transgender category in porn:** Pezzutto, S. and Comella, L. (2020), 'Trans Pornography: Mapping an Emerging Field', *Transgender Studies Quarterly*, 7(2), pp.152–71, http://dx.doi.org/10.1215/23289252-8141985; Pornhub, 'The 2022 Year in Review', https://www.pornhub.com/insights/2022-year-in-review

3   **Children's Commissioner report:** Children's Commissioner (2023), ' "A lot of it is actually just abuse": Young people and pornography', https:// www.childrenscommissioner.gov.uk/wp-content/ uploads/2023/01/cc-a-lot-of-it-is-actually-just-abuse-young-people-and-pornography.pdf

4   **Three porn sites in the top twenty:** Khalili, J. (2021) 'These are the most popular websites right now – and they might just surprise you', TechRadar, https://www.techradar.com/news/ porn-sites-attract-more-visitors-than-netflix-and-amazon-youll-never-guess-how-many. Also in Gesselman, A.N., Kaufman, E.M., Marcotte, A.S., Reynolds, T.A. and Garcia, J.R. (2023) 'Engagement with emerging forms of Sextech: Demographic correlates from a National Sample of Adults in the United States', *Journal of Sex Research*, 60(2), pp.177–89. Similarweb (accessed December 2022; statistics updated monthly), https://www.similarweb.com/top-websites/; **Increase in porn consumption during Covid:** Awan, H.A. et al. (2021), 'Internet and the COVID-19 Pandemic: Presumed Impact and What Can Be Done', *Frontiers in Psychiatry*, https://doi. org/10.3389/fpsyt.2021.623508; Zattoni, F. et al. (2021), 'The impact of COVID-19 pandemic on pornography habits: A global analysis of Google Trends', *International Journal of Impotence Research*, https://doi.org/10.1038/s41443-020-00380-w; Grubbs, J. B. et al. (2022), 'Porndemic?

A Longitudinal Study of Pornography Use Before and During the COVID-19 Pandemic in a Nationally Representative Sample of Americans', *Archives of Sexual Behavior*, https://doi.org/10.1007/s10508-021-02077-7

5 **120 million people visit Pornhub each day:** Pornhub (2020), 'Coronavirus Insights', https://www.pornhub.com/insights/corona-virus

6 **Pornhub site statistics:** Pornhub (2020), 'Coronavirus Insights', https://www.pornhub.com/insights/corona-virus; Pornhub (2021), 'Pornhub's Traffic Increase During the Facebook & Instagram Outage', https://www.pornhub.com/insights/facebook-instagram-outage-2021

7 **Aylo owns over 100 paid-for porn sites:** See entry for MindGeek at thebestporn.com, https://www.thebestporn.com/review_company.html?id=2768; **Playboy.com bought back by Playboy:** Shandrow, K. L. (2014), 'Playboy CEO: Nudity Could Completely Vanish from the Brand', *Entrepreneur*, https://www.entrepreneur.com/starting-a-business/playboy-ceo-nudity-could-completely-vanish-from-the-brand/240346

8 **Porn sites tracking user data:** Maris, E., Libert, T. and Henrichsen, J. R. (2020), 'Tracking sex: The implications of widespread sexual data leakage and tracking on porn websites', *New Media & Society*, 22(11), pp.2018–38, https://doi.org/10.1177/1461444820924632

9 **Surveillance capitalism:** Zuboff, S. (2019), *The Age of Surveillance Capitalism: The Fight for a Human Future at the New Frontier of Power*, Profile Books

10 **Average time on Pornhub:** Pornhub (2016), 'The Long and Short of Porn Watching', https://www.pornhub.com/insights/long-short-porn-watching

11 **Pornhub on women:** Broderick, R. (2014), '14 Things You Might Not Know About How Women Watch Porn', Buzzfeed, https://www.buzzfeed.com/ryanhatesthis/how-women-watch-porn; Pornhub (2021), '2021 Year in Review', https://www.pornhub.com/insights/yir-2021; **Niki Davis-Fainbloom:** Pornhub (2021), 'What Women Like to Watch', https://www.pornhub.com/insights/demographics; https://www.pornhub.com/insights/2022-year-in-review

12 **Feminist pornography critiquing Pornhub:** Gilmour, P. (2020), 'Women who watch porn have better sex', *Cosmopolitan*, 9 October 2020, https://www.cosmopolitan.com/uk/love-sex/sex/a34327568/women-porn-effects-sex/; Lust, E. (2020), '*New York Times*, Pornhub, Visa & Mastercard: The Debate', *Erika Says*, https://erikalust.com/lustzine/voices/newyorktimes-pornhub-investigation

13 **Billie Eilish on pornography:** BBC (2021), 'Billie Eilish says porn exposure while young caused nightmares', BBC News, 14 December 2021, https://www.bbc.co.uk/news/entertainment-arts-59658663; Turner, G. (2021), 'Billie Eilish Goes on

Stigmatizing Anti-Porn Tirade on Howard Stern's Show', *Xbiz*, 14 December 2021, https://www.xbiz.com/news/263603/billie-eilish-goes-on-stigmatizing-anti-porn-tirade-on-howard-sterns-show

DESIRE

1   **Nancy Friday 'meeting and mating':** Gates, A. (2017), 'Nancy Friday, 84, Best-Selling Student of Gender Politics, Dies', *New York Times*, 5 November 2017, https://www.nytimes.com/2017/11/05/obituaries/nancy-friday-84-best-selling-student-of-gender-politics-dies.html

2   *Cosmopolitan* **claims 'women don't have fantasies':** Dubberley, E. (2014), *Garden of Desires: The Evolution of Women's Sexual Fantasies*, Random House.

3   **Pornhub statistics on what women watch:** Pornhub (2014), 'What Women Want', https://www.pornhub.com/insights/what-women-want; Pornhub (2019), 'Women of the World', https://www.pornhub.com/insights/women-of-the-world; Pornhub (2022), 'The 2022 Year in Review', https://www.pornhub.com/insights/2022-year-in-review

4   **Women watching gay male porn:** Pornhub (2017), 'Girls Who Like Boys Who Like Boys', https://www.pornhub.com/insights/girls-like-boys-who-like-boys

5   **Health benefits of sex:** Diamond, L. M. and Huebner, D. M. (2012), 'Is good sex good for you? Rethinking sexuality and health', *Social and Personality Psychology Compass*, 6(1), pp.54–69, https://doi.org/10.1111/j.1751-9004.2011.00408.x

6   ***Marie Claire* porn survey:** De Cadenet, A. (2015), 'More Women Watch (and Enjoy) Porn Than You Ever Realized: A *Marie Claire* Study', *Marie Claire*, https://www.marieclaire.com/sex-love/a16474/women-porn-habits-study/

7   **Women's fantasies of being dominated:** Critelli, J. W. and Bivona, J. M. (2008), 'Women's Erotic Rape Fantasies: An Evaluation of Theory and Research', *Journal of Sex Research*, 45(1), pp.57–70, https://doi.org/10.1080/00224490701808191

8   ***Fifty Shades of Grey:*** Irvine, C. (2012), 'Sir Salman Rushdie: "Fifty Shades of Grey makes Twilight look like War and Peace"', *The Telegraph*, 9 October 2012, https://www.telegraph.co.uk/culture/books/booknews/9596577/Sir-Salman-Rushdie-Fifty-Shades-of-Grey-makes-Twilight-look-like-War-and-Peace.html; James, E. L. (2011), *Fifty Shades of Grey*, Vintage.

9   **Fantasies of submission and domination:** Bivona, J. M., Critelli, J. W. and Clark, M. J. (2012), 'Women's Rape Fantasies: An Empirical Evaluation of the Major Explanations', *Archives of Sexual Behavior*, 41(5), pp.1107–19, https://doi.

org/10.1007/s10508-012-9934-6; Joyal, C. C., Cossette, A. and Lapierre, V. (2015), 'What Exactly Is an Unusual Sexual Fantasy?', *The Journal of Sexual Medicine*, 12(2), pp.328–40, https://doi.org/10.1111/jsm.12734

10 **Panicked arousal:** Garner, M. (2016), *Conflicts, contradictions, and commitments: Men speak about sexualisation of culture*, PhD thesis, London Metropolitan University

11 **Tracking on Pornhub:** Rama, I. et al. (2022), 'The platformization of gender and sexual identities: An algorithmic analysis of Pornhub', *Porn Studies*, pp.1–20, https://doi.org/10.1080/23268743.2022.2066566

12 **Reith lectures on AI:** Russell, S. (2021), 'The Biggest Event in Human History', *BBC Reith Lecture Series: Living with Artifical Intelligence*, https://www.bbc.co.uk/programmes/m001216j

BODIES

1 **Mistaking the vagina for the vulva:** Waldersee, V. (2019), 'Half of Brits don't know where the vagina is – and it's not just the men', YouGov, https://yougov.co.uk/topics/health/articles-reports/2019/03/08/half-brits-dont-know-where-vagina-and-its-not-just; **Difficulty in locating the clitoris:** Geddes, L. (2021), 'Most Britons cannot name all parts of the vulva, survey reveals', *Guardian*, https://www.theguardian.com/lifeandstyle/2021/

may/30/most-britons-cannot-name-parts-vulva-survey; **Half of US women can't identify the cervix or the uterus:** Bremner, J. (2020), 'Quarter of women in America don't know where their vagina is, survey finds', *Independent*, https://www.independent.co.uk/life-style/vagina-reproduction-women-us-education-b1720217.html

2 **Porn's relationship to body dissatisfaction:** Paslakis, G., Chiclana Actis, C. and Mestre-Bach, G. (2022), 'Associations between pornography exposure, body image and sexual body image: A systematic review', *Journal of Health Psychology*, 27(3), pp.743–60, https://doi.org/10.1177/1359105320967085

3 **Natalie Portman on *Black Swan* masturbation scene:** 'Natalie Portman Talks "Black Swan" Masturbation Scene', MTV, 30 November 2010, https://www.mtv.com/news/64j8jp/natalie-portman-talks-black-swan-masturbation-scene

4 **Most women assume other women penetrate themselves:** Fahs, B. and Frank, E. (2014), 'Notes from the Back Room: Gender, Power, and (In)Visibility in Women's Experiences of Masturbation', *The Journal of Sex Research*, 51(3), pp.241–52, https://doi.org/10.1080/00224499.2012.745474

5 **Pornhub's statement for 'Blackout Tuesday':** Pornhub (2020), Twitter post, https://twitter.com/Pornhub/status/1266929094329016325?s=20&t=

PFgD_v-kuLeO7NEUKLRTGQ; **Yomi Adegoke on racism and porn:** Adegoke, Y. (2019) 'Why are people silent about the abuses and exploitation in porn?', *Guardian*, https://www.theguardian.com/commentisfree/2019/aug/15/why-are-people-silent-about-the-abuses-and-exploitation-in-porn

SEX

1   **Sex as a problem for women:** Moore, S. (2015), '8 reasons you're not orgasming', *Cosmopolitan*, https://www.cosmopolitan.com/sex-love/news/a49078/why-cant-i-have-an-orgasm/; Pantony, A. (2021), 'No libido, no problem. Here's how to increase your sex drive, according to a doctor', *Glamour UK*, 30 June 2021

2   **Paris Hilton, 'I may be sexy':** Quoted in Heldman, C. (2010), 'Raunch Culture Is Not Empowering', *Ms Magazine*, 15 March 2010, https://msmagazine.com/2010/03/15/prude/

3   **Bea Campbell on frigidity:** Campbell, B. (1980), 'A feminist sexual politics: Now you see it, now you don't', *Feminist Review*, 5(1), pp.1–18, https://doi.org/10.1057/fr.1980

4   **Parallels between language of porn and Incels:** Tranchese, A. and Sugiura, L. (2021), ' "I Don't Hate All Women, Just Those Stuck-Up Bitches": How Incels and Mainstream Pornography Speak the Same *Extreme* Language of Misogyny',

Violence Against Women, 27(14), pp.2709–34, https://doi.org/10.1177/10778012221996453

5   **Study on online misogyny:** Demos (2016), *The Use of Misogynistic Terms on Twitter*, https://demosuk. wpengine.com/wp-content/uploads/2016/05/ Misogyny-online.pdf

6   **3AM model of sexual socialization:** Wright, P. J. (2011), 'Mass Media Effects On Youth Sexual Behavior Assessing the Claim for Causality', *Annals of the International Communication Association*, 35(1), pp.343–85, https://doi.org/10. 1080/23808985.2011.11679121

7   **Young people using porn as sex education:** Cheney, K., Kamusiime, A. and Mekonnen Yimer, A. (2017), 'Feeling "Blue": Pornography and Sex Education in Eastern Africa', *IDS Bulletin*, 48(1), pp.81–97, https://repub.eur.nl/ pub/108716/; Lothian-McLean, M. (2019), 'How do your porn habits compare with young people across Britain?', BBC Three, 14 March 2019, https://www.bbc.co.uk/bbcthree/article/bb79a2ce-0de4-4965-98f0-9ebbcfcc2a60; Children's Commissioner (2023), '"A lot of it is actually abuse": Young people and pornography', https:// www.childrenscommissioner.gov.uk/wp-content/ uploads/2023/01/cc-a-lot-of-it-is-actually-just-abuse-young-people-and-pornography.pdf

8   **Benefits of young people using porn:** Quadara, A., El-Murr, A. and Latham, J. (2017), 'The effects of pornography on children and young people',

Australian Institute of Family Studies: Melbourne, https://aifs.gov.au/research/research-reports/effects-pornography-children-and-young-people; Harvey, P. (2020), 'Let's Talk About Porn: The Perceived Effect of Online Mainstream Pornography on LGBTQ Youth', *Gender, Sexuality and Race in the Digital Age*, pp.31–52, https://doi.org/10.1007/978-3-030-29855-5_3; Bőthe, B., Vaillancourt-Morel, M. P., Bergeron, S. and Demetrovics, Z. (2019), 'Problematic and non-problematic pornography use among LGBTQ adolescents: A systematic literature review', *Current Addiction Reports*, 6, pp.478–94, https://doi.org/10.1007/s40429-019-00289-5; Attwood, F., Smith, C. and Barker, M. (2018), '"I'm just curious and still exploring myself": Young people and pornography', *New Media & Society*, 20(10), pp.3738–59, https://doi.org/10.1177/1461444818759271

9   **Percentages of men watching porn in the last year:** Romito P. and Beltramini L. (2015), 'Factors Associated With Exposure to Violent or Degrading Pornography Among High School Students', *The Journal of School Nursing*, 31(4), pp.280–90, https://doi.org/10.1177/1059840514563313; Rissel, C. et al. (2017), 'A Profile of Pornography Users in Australia: Findings from the Second Australian Study of Health and Relationships', *The Journal of Sex Research*, 54(2), pp.227–40, https://doi.org/10.1080/00224499.2016.1191597;

Eljawad, M.A. et al. (2021), 'Pornography Use Prevalence and Associated Factors in Arab Countries: A Multinational Cross-Sectional Study of 15,027 Individuals', *The Journal of Sexual Medicine*, 18(3), pp.539–48, https://doi.org/10.1016/j.jsxm.2020.12.011; Al Mamun, M. A. et al. (2019), 'Attitudes and Risk Factors of Pornography Consumption Among Bangladeshi University Students: An Exploratory Study', *International Journal of Mental Health Addiction*, 17, pp.323–35, https://doi.org/10.1007/s11469-018-0021-7; Miller, D. J., Raggatt, P. T. and McBain, K. (2020), 'A Literature Review of Studies into the Prevalence and Frequency of Men's Pornography Use', *American Journal of Sexuality Education*, 15(4), pp.502–29, https://doi.org/10.1080/15546128.2020.1831676; Kirk, I. (2022), 'How often do Britons watch porn?', YouGov, 1 July 2022, https://yougov.co.uk/topics/society/articles-reports/2022/07/01/how-often-do-britons-watch-porn

10 **Impact of men's porn use:** Dwulit, A. D. and Rzymski, P. (2019), 'The Potential Associations of Pornography Use with Sexual Dysfunctions: An Integrative Literature Review of Observational Studies', *Journal of Clinical Medicine*, 8(7), https://doi.org/10.3390/jcm8070914; Park, B. Y. et al. (2016), 'Is internet pornography causing sexual dysfunctions? A review with clinical reports', *Behavioral Sciences*, 6(3), https://doi.org/10.3390/bs6030017; Perry, S. L. (2018), 'Pornography Use

and Depressive Symptoms: Examining the Role of Moral Incongruence', *Society and Mental Health*, 8(3), pp.195–213, https://doi.org/10.1177/2156869317728373

11 **Cindy Gallop, founder of MakeLoveNotPorn:** Gallop, C. (2009), 'Make love, not porn', TED Talk, https://www.ted.com/talks/cindy_gallop_make_love_not_porn/transcript

RELATIONSHIPS

1 **Using porn with partner and partner's use:** Kohut, T. et al. (2021), 'But What's Your Partner Up To? Associations Between Relationship Quality and Pornography Use Depend on Contextual Patterns of Use Within the Couple', *Frontiers in Psychology*, https://doi.org/10.3389/fpsyg.2021.661347; Kohut, T., Fisher, W. A. and Campbell, L. (2017), 'Perceived Effects of Pornography on the Couple Relationship: Initial Findings of Open-Ended, Participant-Informed, "Bottom-Up" Research', *Archives of Sexual Behavior*, 46(2), pp.585–602, https://doi.org/10.1007/s10508-016-0783-6; Resch, M. N. and Alderson, K. G. (2014), 'Female Partners of Men Who Use Pornography: Are Honesty and Mutual Use Associated with Relationship Satisfaction?', *Journal of Sex & Marital Therapy*, 40(5), pp.410–24, https://doi.org/10.1080/0092623X.2012.751077; Willoughby, B. J. and Leonhardt, N. D. (2020), 'Behind Closed

Doors: Individual and Joint Pornography Use Among Romantic Couples', *The Journal of Sex Research*, 57(1), pp.77–91, https://doi:10.1080/00224 499.2018.1541440

2   *Marie Claire* porn survey: De Cadenet, A. (2015), 'More Women Watch (and Enjoy) Porn Than You Ever Realized: A *Marie Claire* Study', *Marie Claire*, https://www.marieclaire.com/sex-love/ a16474/women-porn-habits-study/

3   **Women do not regularly use porn with a male partner:** Carroll, J. S. et al. (2017), 'The Porn Gap: Differences in Men's and Women's Pornography Patterns in Couple Relationships', *Journal of Couple & Relationship Therapy*, 16(2), pp.146–63, https://doi.org/10.1080/15332691.2016.1238796

4   **Women using porn as a means to arousal:** Attwood, F. (2018), 'Women's Pornography', in Harrison K. and Ogden C. (eds), *Pornographies: Critical Positions*, University of Chester Press.

5   **Women's sexual secrets:** Fox, H. C. et al. (2021), 'Gender Differences in Sex Secret Disclosure to a Romantic Partner', *Sexuality & Culture*, pp.1–20, https://doi.org/10.1007/s12119-021-09880-3

6   **Women in relationships use porn to enhance their partnered sex lives more than for themselves:** Cooper, A., Galbreath, N. and Becker, M. A. (2004), 'Sex on the Internet: Furthering our Understanding of Men with Online Sexual Problems', *Psychology of Addictive Behaviors*, 18(3), https://doi.org/10.1037/0893-164X.18.3.223; Hald,

G. M., Seaman, C. and Linz, D. (2014), 'Sexuality and Pornography', in Tolman, D. L. et al. (eds), *APA Handbook of Sexuality and Psychology, Vol. 2. Contextual Approaches*, pp.3–35, American Psychological Association; **Pornography as a relationship phenomenon:** Brown, C. C., Carroll, J. S., Yorgason, J. B., Busby, D. M., Willoughby, B. J. and Larson, J. H. (2017), 'A Common-Fate Analysis of Pornography Acceptance, Use, and Sexual Satisfaction Among Heterosexual Married Couples', *Archives of Sexual Behavior*, 46(2), pp.575–84.

7 **Dan Savage on men's porn use:** Savage, D. (2012), 'Do men watch porn?', 'Savage Love' in the *Chicago Reader*, 8 August 2012, https://chicagoreader.com/columns-opinion/do-men-watch-porn/

8 **Impact of porn on couple's sex lives:** Carroll, J. S., Busby, D. M., Willoughby, B. J. and Brown, C. C. (2017), 'The Porn Gap: Differences in Men's and Women's Pornography Patterns in Couple Relationships', *Journal of Couple & Relationship Therapy*, 16(2), pp.146–63, https://doi.org/10.1080/15332691.2016.1238796; Poulsen, F. O., Busby, D. M. and Galovan, A. M. (2013), 'Pornography Use: Who Uses It and How It Is Associated with Couple Outcomes', *Journal of Sex Research*, 50(1), pp.72–83, https://doi.org/10.1080/00224499.2011.648027; Vaillancourt-Morel, M.P. et al. (2020), 'Pornography Use and Romantic Relationships: A Dyadic Daily Diary Study', *Journal of Social and*

Personal Relationships, 37(10–11), pp.2802–21, https://doi/10.1177/0265407520940048; Vaillancourt-Morel, M.P. et al. (2017), 'Profiles of Cyberpornography Use and Sexual Well-Being in Adults', *Journal of Sexual Medicine*, 14(1), pp.78–85, https://doi.org/10.1016/j.jsxm.2016.10.016

VIOLENCE

1   **Pornhub's content removal:** Cole, S. (2020), 'Pornhub Just Purged All Unverified Content From the Platform', *VICE*, 14 December 2020, https://www.vice.com/en/article/jgqjjy/pornhub-suspended-all-unverified-videos-content; Kristof, N. (2020), 'The Children of Pornhub', *New York Times*, https://www.nytimes.com/2020/12/04/opinion/sunday/pornhub-rape-trafficking.html

2   **Tracking the content of mainstream porn:** Vera-Gray, F., McGlynn, C., Kureshi, I. and Butterby, K. (2021), 'Sexual violence as a sexual script in mainstream online pornography', *The British Journal of Criminology*, 61(5), pp.1243–60, https://doi.org/10.1093/bjc/azab035; **Pornhub's response:** BBC (2021), 'Online porn websites promote "sexually violent" videos', BBC News, 5 April 2021, https://www.bbc.co.uk/news/technology-56640178

3   **Violent porn and attitudes condoning violence against women:** Hald, G. M., Malamuth, N. M. and Yuen, C. (2010), 'Pornography and Attitudes

Supporting Violence Against Women: Revisiting the Relationship in Nonexperimental Studies', *Aggressive Behavior: Official Journal of the International Society for Research on Aggression*, 36(1), pp.14–20, https://doi.org/10.1002/ab.20328

4   **Revelations on James Deen:** Grant, M. G. (2015), 'How Stoya took on James Deen and broke the porn industry's silence', *Guardian*, https://www.theguardian.com/culture/2015/dec/04/how-stoya-took-on-james-deen-and-broke-the-porn-industrys-silence; Clark-Flory, T. (2015), '"Help Me": Porn Performers Detail New Allegations Against James Deen', Vocativ, https://www.vocativ.com/news/256579/james-deen-new-allegations/; Innes, C. (2020) 'Why did we ignore porn's #MeToo?', *Cosmopolitan*, https://www.cosmopolitan.com/uk/reports/a30806689/james-deen-porn-me-too/

5   **Claims made about the production company of Erika Lust:** Clark-Flory, T. (2018), 'Is Feminist Porn Getting Its #Metoo Moment?', Jezebel, https://jezebel.com/is-feminist-porn-getting-its-metoo-moment-1828173419; Tamara, Z. (2019), 'Erika Lust Responds to Hello Rooster's "Unethical Sets" Allegations', *XBiz*, https://www.xbiz.com/news/246319/erika-lust-responds-to-hello-roosters-unethical-sets-allegations; Joint statement by Erika Lust Films & Hello Rooster (June 2021), https://erikalust.com/joint-statement

6   **Porn used by men who've murdered women:**
Garber-Paul, E. (2016), 'Flashback: Ted Bundy
Says Porn "Fueled" Him in Bizarre Last
Interview', *Rolling Stone*, 3 October 2016, https://
www.rollingstone.com/culture/culture-news/
flashback-ted-bundy-says-porn-fueled-him-in-
bizarre-last-interview-129458/; McCann, J. (2021),
'Why was Wayne Couzens known as "the rapist"?
Origins of nickname of Sarah Everard's killer
explained', the *i paper*, 3 October 2021, https://
inews.co.uk/news/uk/wayne-couzens-the-rapist-
nickname-why-known-as-sarah-everard-killer-
explained-1227129; Gay, E. (2020), 'Grace
Millane's killer searched for extreme pornography
moments after murder', 23 December 2020, Stuff,
https://www.stuff.co.nz/national/crime/300186217/
grace-millanes-killer-searched-for-extreme-
pornography-moments-after-murder

7   **Rape resulting in physical response:** Shin, H. J.
and Salter, M. (2022), 'Betrayed by my body:
Survivor experiences of sexual arousal and
psychological pleasure during sexual violence',
Journal of Gender-Based Violence, 6(3), pp.581–95,
https://doi.org/10.1332/239868021X16430290699192

8   **The Clit List:** Oppenheim, M. (2015), 'Meet the
Activist Behind the UK's First Clinic for Women
Trying to Reclaim Their Bodies After Being
Raped', *VICE*, 29 May 2015, https://www.vice.
com/en/article/wd75qw/reclaiming-your-body-
after-sexual-assault-172; Amara, P. (2017), 'What

running the UK's first maternity clinic for rape victims has taught me about violence against women', *The Telegraph*, https://www.telegraph.co.uk/women/life/running-uks-first-maternity-clinic-rape-victims-has-taught-violence/

9   **Survivors of violence watching porn:** Cascalheira, C. J. et al. (2021), 'Curative Kink: Survivors of Early Abuse Transform Trauma Through BDSM', *Sexual and Relationship Therapy*, pp.1–31, https://doi.org/10.1080/14681994.2021.1937599; Romito, P. and Beltramini, L. (2011), 'Watching Pornography: Gender Differences, Violence and Victimization. An Exploratory Study in Italy', *Violence Against Women*, 17(10), pp.1313–26, https://doi.org/10.1177/107780121142455

FUTURE

1   **Epic Games investing in the metaverse:** Tassi, P. (2022), 'Fortnite's Epic Games Makes a Metaverse Investment to Scale Up Even Further', *Forbes*, https://www.forbes.com/sites/paultassi/2022/09/23/fortnites-epic-games-makes-a-metaverse-investment-to-scale-up-even-further/?sh=4f0f50972cfd

2   **DreamCam on the metaverse:** Edwards, C. (2022), 'Love online: Virtual reality "exoskeleton" will aid futuristic sex in the metaverse, expert reveals', the *Sun*, 15 March 2022, https://www.thesun.co.uk/tech/17961195/metaverse-sex-virtual-reality-exoskeleton-dreamtouch/

3   **Corey Price from Pornhub:** Corey Price from
    Pornhub quoted in *Express & Star* (2018),
    'Pornhub is now accepting cryptocurrency to offer
    anonymous payments', *Express & Star*, 18 April
    2018, https://www.expressandstar.com/news/
    science-and-technology/2018/04/18/pornhub-is-
    now-accepting-cryptocurrency-to-offer-
    anonymous-payments/; **Does Corey Price exist?**
    Coffee, P. (2020), 'Pornhub has been widely
    covered for its marketing savvy. But its most-
    quoted executives are nearly invisible, and it's
    unclear if they actually exist', *Business Insider*, 16
    December 2020, https://www.businessinsider.com/
    pornhub-and-the-popular-sites-mysterious-
    executives-2020-9?r=US&IR=T

4   **Statistics on VR porn:** VRporn (2017) 'VR porn
    and the web: A statistical study', Vrporn, https://
    vrporn.com/vr-porn-and-the-web-a-statistical-
    study/; Sex-tech guide (2021), 'Majority of US and
    UK VR users have watched porn on their
    headsets', Sextechguide, https://sextechguide.com/
    vr/majority-us-uk-watched-adult-vr/

5   **Female VR users experienced sexual harassment
    in VR worlds:** Outlaw, J. and Duckles, B. (2017),
    'Why Women Don't Like Social Virtual Reality:
    A Study of Safety, Usability, and Self-Expression
    in Social VR', The Extended Mind, https://www.
    extendedmind.io/why-women-dont-like-social-
    virtual-reality

6 **Female researcher raped in Meta's VR platform:** Basu, T. (2021), 'The metaverse has a groping problem already', *MIT Technology Review*, 16 December 2021, https://www.technologyreview.com/2021/12/16/1042516/the-metaverse-has-a-groping-problem/

7 **Girl's avatar raped in Roblox hack:** Perez, S. (2018), 'Roblox responds to the hack that allowed a child's avatar to be raped in its game', Tech Crunch, 18 July 2018, https://techcrunch.com/2018/07/18/roblox-responds-to-the-hack-that-allowed-a-childs-avatar-to-be-raped-in-its-game

8 **Roblox used to sexually groom children:** Clayton, J. and Dyer, J. (2022), 'Roblox: The children's game with a sex problem', BBC News, 15 February 2022, https://www.bbc.co.uk/news/technology-60314572

9 **Researcher on being sexually assaulted on VR venues:** Patel, N. J. (2021), 'Reality or Fiction?', Medium, 21 December 2021, https://medium.com/kabuni/fiction-vs-non-fiction-98aa0098f3b0

10 **British attitudes survey:** NatCen (2017), https://www.bsa.natcen.ac.uk/media/39147/bsa34_moral_issues_final.pdf

11 **BBFC study on young people and porn:** British Board of Film Classification (2019), 'New research commissioned by the BBFC into the impact of pornography on children demonstrates significant

support for age-verification', BBFC, https://www.bbfc.co.uk/about-us/news/children-see-pornography-as-young-as-seven-new-report-finds

12 **France digital verification:** Samuel, H. (2023), 'France to force pornography viewers to prove their age with "digital certificate"', the *Telegraph*, https://www.telegraph.co.uk/world-news/2023/02/06/france-force-pornography-viewers-prove-age-digital-certificate/

13 **David Cameron porn announcement:** https://www.gov.uk/government/speeches/the-internet-and-pornography-prime-minister-calls-for-action

14 **'Simple and secure solution':** AgeID, https://www.ageid.com/

15 **Audre Lorde:** Lorde, A. (2017), 'The Uses of the Erotic', *Your Silence Will Not Protect You*, Silver Press, pp.22–30, quote from page 24.

AFTERWORD

1 https://www.bbc.co.uk/news/world-europe-66877718